The Bigger they are - the harder they fall

(Overcoming [illegible]ts)

The Bigger they are - the harder they fall

Discovering the enemy's methods in
the giant nations God promised to drive out of the
promised land

"Here is how you shall know that the living God
is among you and that he will
without fail drive out from before you
the Canaanites, the Hittites, the Hivites,
the Perizzites, the Girgashites,
the Amorites, and the Jebusites."

For Bethan, Owen and Ffion

The Bigger they are - the harder they fall (Overcoming giants)

Paperback: ISBN 978-1-914408-82-3

This edition October 2021.

Layout and design by the author

Published under Biddles Books.

Distributed from 1 Sulby Close, Spalding, PE11 3QS

Typeset in Palatino 11pt/14pt.

Dedication

I dedicate this work to the men and women who sat under my ministry for 20 years at New Street Baptist Church. I will be for ever grateful for their willingness to invite me to serve them, and for their faithfulness over the years. They made me study deeper into the things of God, and in many ways made my ministry, under God, all that it became.

I also want to thank and acknowledge a man who started out as a role model at a distance for me, and over the years became a friend, a mentor, and ultimately a father to me in the things of God.

Bishop Kenneth C Ulmer, you challenged me, made me delve into my heart and soul, examine the Scriptures and test my convictions and traditions against the touchstone of the truth of the Word of God. I thank God for you, and remember with heartfelt thanks your willingness to watch over me and minister among us at New Street.

My grateful thanks also to Judith for all the help and encouragement in ministry, in getting this finished and corrected, and in my life. You are my love, my heart beat. I thank God for you.

Unless otherwise mentioned quotations from the scriptures are taken from the English Standard Version or the Authorised Version of the Bible.

Table of contents

Here is how you shall know that the living God is among you and that he will without fail drive out from before you the Canaanites, the Hittites, the Hivites, the Perizzites, the Girgashites, the Amorites, and the Jebusites. Joshua 3:9-10

Preface

> *"Behold, the days are coming," declares the Lord God, "when I will send a famine on the land—not a famine of bread, nor a thirst for water, but of hearing the words of the Lord. They shall wander from sea to sea, and from north to east; they shall run to and fro, to seek the word of the Lord, but they shall not find it.*

I sometimes wonder whether I have been born into the kind of day the prophet Amos spoke of, when he prophesied saying God would send a famine on the land, a famine not of bread, nor a thirst for water, but of hearing the words of the Lord. Days when you would be able to run to and fro seeking the word of the Lord in vain.

The days I live in are certainly strange days in many ways. They are days when there has been an explosion in the proliferation of Bible versions available. There are not only translations and paraphrases, but a vast array of 'so called' thematic versions.

Yet it seems to me that I live in days where fewer and fewer people seem to know, study and meditate upon the scriptures and where the notion of simple biblical teaching, with the aim of explaining and expounding the meaning of the word of God, is uncommon.

For all the truth that people have a vast number of Bibles, it seems that many are rarely opened, and sadly where they are opened they are read with little comprehension of the spiritual reality and truth they have before them in the very spoken Word of God.

Instead of straightforward Bible understanding, all too often the people I have been among, neither know the stories of the Old Testament, nor yet have any concept of their relevance to spiritual life in the 21st Century.

We claim to follow the Lord Jesus, the Christ of God, who spoke of the scriptures, as the unchanging and inerrant Word of God. It was Jesus who said that all of the Scriptures speak of Him. Yet when He said that, He was speaking primarily of the Old Testament. There was nothing beyond that in His day. But oh, how rarely are those books read, how rarely are they opened, and how rarely does anyone appear to find Jesus, or the way to life, within those pages.

I seem to have lived among those who only ever turn to the New Testament, as though they contain the only true Scripture. In so doing we may miss the unity and beauty of the whole of the Bible, let alone become aware of the spiritual forces which are at work in the world.

In reading only the New Testament we are in danger of gaining only shallow understanding of God's plan and purpose. Such a concentration only on the New Testament mingled with a way of seeing it primarily with a view centred on the modern material and temporal world, has tended towards a failure of grasping the whole counsel of God, as the pictures, the references, and the shadows from the Old Testament, are at best overlooked, or in some cases completely redefined.

Whenever Jesus opened up the Scriptures to His disciples, whenever the Apostles preached the gospel, they were opening the Hebrew Bible, to speak of Jesus, of the life which comes from knowing God, and the struggles and full blessings of the spiritual realm.

Instead of people digging deep into the word for life and sustenance, we seem to have become a people who know little, understand less, and are only ever aware of some skimpy surface idea of the person of the living God, and the awful state that man's sin has created as revealed in the Scriptures.

In an attempt to, at least in my own small way, rectify this famine, I release these studies. They represent much of my aim and ministry, to show the unity of the teaching of God, running from Genesis to Revelation.

It is my contention that the whole of the Bible is a single, unified teaching, outlining the purpose and plan of the living God. It is a plan where God comes and reaches out to a lost humanity, and shows His power over the evil one, and set out the method He will use to bring that humanity, spoiled and tricked by Satan, back into a relationship with Himself. It declares God's plan and purpose for each one of us, that by restoring our relationship with Him, He plans to use us to make the wonder of true worship, and the joy of meaningful relationship with Him, known to the rest of the world, until the day when the whole earth is filled with the glory of God, as the waters cover the sea.

I hope these pages will enlighten and challenge the reader,

but more than that, it is my prayer, they will inspire the reader to take the time to read, study, meditate and rejoice in the wonder of the totality of the holy scriptures, which scriptures are able to make us wise unto salvation. From that, my earnest desire is to see a return to a time where people are being fed with the very bread of life, the Word of God, both the written word and that word revealed in Jesus the Christ.

I commend this book to you, but above all, I commend the Scriptures to each reader, and pray God will illumine His Word, in our hearts and minds, by the power of the Holy Spirit, and for the exalting of the majestic and mighty name of Jesus the Christ.

David S Williams
Spalding
October 2021

The Bigger they are - the harder they fall

"Here is how you shall know that the living God
is among you and that he will
without fail drive out from before you
the Canaanites, the Hittites, the Hivites,
the Perizzites, the Girgashites,
the Amorites, and the Jebusites."

Giants in the land

> *"When the Lord your God brings you into the land that you are entering to take possession of it, and clears away many nations before you, the Hittites, the Girgashites, the Amorites, the Canaanites, the Perizzites, the Hivites, and the Jebusites, seven nations more numerous and mightier than you, and when the Lord your God gives them over to you, and you defeat them, then you must devote them to complete destruction. You shall make no covenant with them and show no mercy to them. You shall not intermarry with them, giving your daughters to their sons or taking their daughters for your sons, for they would turn away your sons from following me, to serve other gods. Then the anger of the Lord would be kindled against you, and he would destroy you quickly. But thus shall you deal with them: you shall break down their altars and dash in pieces their pillars and chop down their Asherim and burn their carved images with fire. "For you are a people holy to the Lord your God. The Lord your God has chosen you to be a people for his treasured possession, out of all the peoples who are on the face of the earth.*
> *Deuteronomy 7:1-6*

The account of the exodus of the people of God, when they were delivered from captivity and bondage, together with their wilderness wanderings and the eventual arrival into the land of promise, has always been a highlight of the Old Testament narrative. It is a highlight not only because of the reality of the wonders that God performed for the people back in those days, but also as a picture, a shadow of the deliverance which is still offered to people, through the shed blood, death and resurrection of Jesus the Christ.

All too often, though, when that shadow is taught or considered, the entry into the land of promise is thought of only in terms of the eternal rest of God's people. The danger of that interpretation as the only lesson of spiritual significance in the account, is the way in which the land was taken little by little, by conquest in battle, and the overcoming of the enemies which stood in the way of the people of God. It is my hope, and the evidence of Biblical teaching, that when we reach the eternal realm, and the presence of our glorious God, all battles and struggles will cease, and our entry will be to a place of bliss, rest and joy in the fullness of God's presence, and the opportunity to worship without the interference of sin, or the struggles of this world.

It may well be that there is a whole other way of reading the journey and the struggles to be overcome on the way into the land of promise, where the wilderness is our place of discovering the blessing of obedience, and our entry into the land of promise speaks of our discovering that God has set a store of promises which He has given in order to allow us to live, even here, in a place where we may know His favour and blessing resting upon us.

It is the Apostle Peter who writes in 2 Peter 1:3-4

> *His divine power has granted to us all things that pertain to life and godliness, through the*

> *knowledge of him who called us to his own glory and excellence, by which he has granted to us his precious and very great promises, so that through them you may become partakers of the divine nature, having escaped from the corruption that is in the world because of sinful desire.*

As the people of God wandered in the wilderness, Moses sent a group of spies to look over the land of promise and see what it was like. It was an expeditionary mission to the land which God had promised to give to them. One spy from each of the twelve tribes was commissioned to go. When the spies returned they reported on how very great were the blessings of the land which God had promised to give them. Their report is recorded in Numbers 13:27 and following.

> *"We came to the land.... It flows with milk and honey, and this is its fruit."*

Ten of the spies reported on the problems of receiving the land, drawing attention to the struggles, instead of the blessings that awaited them. Neither did they mention the promise God had made to give the land to His people.

> *"However, the people who dwell in the land are strong, and the cities are fortified and very large. And besides, we saw the descendants of Anak there. The Amalekites dwell in the land of the Negeb. The Hittites, the Jebusites, and the Amorites dwell in the hill country. And the Canaanites dwell by the sea, and along the Jordan."*

Then finally they are recorded as saying:

> *"We are not able to go up against the people, for they are stronger than we are. The land, through which we have gone to spy it out, is a land that devours its inhabitants, and all the people that we saw in it are of great height. And there we saw the Nephilim (the sons of Anak, who come from the Nephilim), and we seemed to ourselves like grasshoppers, and so we seemed to them."*

Their claim was, that the land was full of nations of people who were bigger, greater and stronger than the people of God.

Only Caleb and Joshua drew attention to the fact of God's promise, and the certainty that, with God on their side, no giant has the power to overcome and destroy them. Moses and Aaron supported the view of Caleb and Joshua in these remarkable words in chapter 14:7-9

> *"The land, which we passed through to spy it out, is an exceedingly good land. If the Lord delights in us, he will bring us into this land and give it to us, a land that flows with milk and honey. Only do not rebel against the Lord. And do not fear the people of the land, for they are bread for us. Their protection is removed from them, and the Lord is with us; do not fear them."*

The people rebelled against God, refusing to walk in obedience or into the promises that God had given to them. The whole nation then wandered for years, never receiving the promises.

Towards the end of the life of Moses, as he is handing over

the leadership of God's people to Joshua, he comes and speaks again of the truth that God intended to take His people into a place of promise, a place of favour and a place of blessing, but that to obtain the land of promise the people would need to overcome seven nations of giants.

As Moses speaks of those seven nations, he declares that God will drive the nations out of the land before His people. He acknowledges that the seven nations, were indeed nations of giants, but then moves on to give some instruction on how the people are to deal with those nations of giants, as God drives them out of the land before them.

Moses declares that God will drive the giants out, but at the same time God's people had a responsibility before God in the way they then dealt with those giant nations.

Once Joshua had taken over the leadership, and Moses has entered into the eternal rest of God, Joshua comes to speak to the people of God. He is recorded as saying:

> *"Come here and listen to the words of the Lord your God. Here is how you shall know that the living God is among you and that he will without fail drive out from before you the Canaanites, the Hittites, the Hivites, the Perizzites, the Girgashites, the Amorites, and the Jebusites." Joshua 3:9-10*

Like Moses, Joshua draws attention to the seven nations of giants who inhabit the land of promise, but this time Joshua adds an extra dimension. He says that the evidence of the presence of God among His people will be seen in the victories the people gain over these nations.

Now, I don't know if you have ever wondered about that list of nations, the seven nations of giants who are going to attempt to stop the people living in the blessing of the land of promise.

It may be that you have read their names and skated over them, thinking they are just names used to fill up the page, and added for no great reason.

That is never my view of the Scripture. It is my contention that every word is there for a reason, and every word is profitable. More than that, when God takes the time to repeat something, I believe we owe it to our spiritual well-being to stop, study and seek to understand what God is saying for our benefit. In addition names in the Bible frequently have a meaning within them which is often the source of benefit and instruction, if we take the time to study that meaning out.

I want to show, over these pages, that the names of these seven nations of giants, relate to seven attitudes of heart, seven modes of thought, seven lifestyles, seven paradigms which the enemy of souls, and the world system will try to use to mould and conform our minds to their will. If we are not careful this will keep us from inheriting the benefit of the promises of God, and keep us from becoming the holy individuals God desires of His covenant people.

Each of these nation's names refers to a different attitude

which will try to stop us entering fully into receiving the benefit of those precious and very great promises which God has given to us. Each mindset will attempt to stop us become partakers of the divine nature, and seek to keep us in a wilderness of disobedience, wandering from God, and governed by the zeitgeist of this world and it's rulerships.

Over the next chapters, I want to invite you to join me on a journey of discovery looking at these seven giant nations that the Lord has promised to drive out before us. As we look at the name of each nation we will discover that every one refers to an attitude of heart and mind still common today.

In the same way, that God led his people out of bondage, through the Red Sea, into the wilderness, and into the promised land, all those years ago, there are still many of His children, stuck in the place of bondage. God wants to lead us all out of bondage. There are some of His people, who have been led out of bondage, but are still wandering around in a wilderness, struggling with the concept that the God who saved them is also the God who desires to be the Lord of all they are. They just haven't got very much further, than experiencing the initial loosening of the bondage and captivity of sin and Satan. Finally, there are many of us who have made our way towards the land of promise, and are struggling with battles and trials as we seek to inherit every promise God has set down in His word to enable us to live in the fullness of His blessing here and now.

God wants us to live with the ability to start each and

every day saying, I am the favoured of the Lord, I am the blessed of the Lord, I'm walking in the blessing of the Lord. His declared will is that day by day we might see Him fulfilling His promises to us, arriving at the end of each day, still knowing the favour of God upon us. Maybe weary, but victorious in our living for Him, and engaged in the worship and adoration of His name for all He is and all He continues to do for us, in us and with us.

We need to realise and remember that every promise in God's word is not just for somebody else, it is not just for the person living next to us, it is written for us. He gave the promises that we might inherit them, that we might be partakers of them, and walk in the blessing of them. Every promise in the word is not simply for us, they are truly Yea, and Amen in Jesus the Christ, to the glory of God. He gives these promises, not just for our blessing, but in order for glory to come to the name of our triune, ineffable God.

The problem is this. When we come to try and walk in His promises, there are a number of things that will stop us receiving the promises. The things that are going to stop us receiving the promises, the bulk of the issues and barriers to receiving the fulfilment of every word God has declared, are found here, in the name of these seven giants. They are summed up in the battles we face with Hittites, Girgashites, Amorites, Canaanites, Perizzites, Hivites, and Jebusites. Every one of those nations will come against us, to seek to stop us receiving all that God has prepared for us, in order that we walk in His blessing.

But we must notice and realise something significant

about what God says in overcoming these giants. First, God says, I'm going to drive out those nations. Now, when we read that, we could be tempted to think that all we have to do is sit and wait for God to overcome the difficulties, and that we have nothing to do except wait for God to do His thing.

That would be quite wrong. We need to realise that is not what God says. Yes, He declares He will give us these nations. Yes, He says He will give us the victory. But then He declares that we have a responsibility to rid ourselves of them, of their presence, of their influence, and of their attempts to infiltrate our minds. We must put each of these ways of thinking to death, to refuse to allow them access to the way we think. God declares, He will give us all we need to be victorious but we have to take the attitude, the mindset, the lifestyle that seeks to keep us from becoming a holy people, inheriting the promises and rid our hearts and minds of each one of them.

When we seek to rid ourselves of these giant attitudes, we must realise that each one is bigger, stronger and more powerful than we are. We will never overcome them by ourselves in our own strength, but with God, all things are possible. Yes we must realise the giants are bigger than us, stronger than us, greater than us and more frightening than us. But when we stand with the omnipotent God and stand against these giants, there is one more thing we ought to remember. The bigger they are, the harder they fall, and fall they will.

There is victory to be won, we can be overcomers, we can be more than conquerors, all the time God is with us and is the source of our life and the dependency of our days. We can destroy the spirit of the age as it seeks to keep us from God. We can come against it and destroy it by bringing every thought into the captivity of Christ.

> *We destroy arguments and every lofty opinion raised against the knowledge of God, and take every thought captive to obey Christ, being ready to punish every disobedience, when your obedience is complete. 2 Corinthians 10 5-6*

As we look at the names of these nations, remember, God says we have to destroy all they represent and stand for.

God adds something else as Moses gives the information of these nations and the instruction of how to deal with them in our lives. Moses says, when we come and see one of these giants (and God allows the giant to be in our way in order that with Him we come and destroy it) whatever we do, we must not get into a conversation with them. We must not start to discuss things with them. We dare not try to make an agreement or covenant with them, or let them persuade us to enter into a league with him.

That is not because God is a bloodthirsty God. It's just that God knows if we start to try and discuss things with these giants, they are cleverer than we are, they are subtle, they are scheming liars. We may think we are clever and will win the argument, but we are not that clever. We may think we can allow them to coexist with us, it is the path to defeat and failure. The giant will win and turn us away from the sweetness of fellowship and communion with the living God.

Let me just give you one example. One of the giants we will discover in this list, is the giant of terror. You know, when we get scared, we try and reason it out.

There are times when I am lying in bed in the middle of the night and hear a noise. I am sure I locked the door. I know I locked the door. Nobody can get in, the windows are shut, maybe even the windows are locked, and I can reason it out to the point where I know I should not be anxious. How many of you know, when you start to reason that kind of situation out, it doesn't make any difference? All you actually do is wake up. God says don't argue with the fear, it's pointless. You'll never win. Rather declare the truth of God against the fear.

Then God says, as well as not making a Covenant with these nations personally, do not let your children get involved with them. God adds this because, the more space you allow the giant to take over in your life, in your home, in your family, the worse your situation is likely to become and the harder you will find it to inherit and walk in the promises God has for you.

Learn instead to walk in the promises. Walk into the promise and declare the truth that every place you stand on, God has promised to give you. You know the old song "I'm standing on the promises of God".

Then God says if we enter into a discussion with these giants something else goes on. If we start to get involved with them, there's something that will always transpire. The giant we have not destroyed will become a snare to us. They will become a snare to keep us from the known and felt presence of the living God.

Moses says they will become a 'snare to keep you. . .'. We don't need reminding what a snare is but the hebrew word used in the phrase 'to keep you' is a word that can be translated as "to turn you off".

God says that the aim of the giant is to "turn us off from Him". These giants, these attitudes, these ways of thinking are all aimed at turning us off of God, of loosing interest in Him, of thinking of Him in the wrong way. They will try to make us think that God is boring, that walking in faith is wearisome, that the way of life offered by the giant is better, more exciting, more interesting, more fun, that the life we find in God.

Have you ever sat late at night, and flicked around the television channels trying to find something that's less boring to watch? You know what happens, you finish up choosing the best of a bad lot. You watch for a while and then, in the end, you turn that off and get to sleep. Because at least that's not as boring.

We will notice that one of the aims of these giants is to bring a boredom into our life, to turn us off of God. Another will be to ensure fear comes into our lives to turn us off of God. Another one is to make us settle for low attitudes that take over our life to turn us off of God. A further aim is to bring a lack of vision and purpose into life and this will, in turn take us away from enjoying God.

Then, when we are turned off of God, we forget His promises. We are turned off from God, and we forget His word, and we quickly cease to walk in blessing. Then, it appears quite suddenly, life is a mess. We think "why is my life a mess?" God says "I can tell you why it is a mess, you let a giant steal the promise that was yours. I let the giant be there, but I gave you the tools to get rid of it. I said this word can kill it and you said oh, okay. But instead of killing it, you thought you would try something different, something which appeared to be easier, but nothing else will ever work."

What giant will you struggle to slay, because you are not in a place where God is speaking to you. He has given us the tools, to rid ourselves of each giant. He says He wants us to know what will happen if we will not refuse to make a league with them.

Understand God allows these giants to come into our lives for a reason. He wants to lead us into blessing, He wants us to become stronger in our faith as we follow Him. All that He does for one reason alone. The reason isn't because we were so incredibly wonderful all by ourselves. It is just because God chose to love us. I don't know why, but God says He just chose to love us and because He loves us He chooses to bless us and He chooses to bless us just for His own glory.

His purpose is simple. He will watch us walk along in life, and then suddenly something will happen as we are walking along. A giant appears and we will be struck with how large this giant is. The giant comes to try and take us away from God. We look at it and think, "what on earth can I do, how can I ever cope with this?" God says, "when you start to look at the giant and wonder whether you get through that problem; through that difficulty and inherit the promise? When you wonder whether you are able to stop what is coming against you to take you away from the living God. Remember me." He says "Remember, you can not get through the problem alone. You can not overcome the difficulty. you are not able to slay the giant alone, because they are bigger and stronger than you. But remember you are not, and never will be, alone."

We remember God, because the God who is with us and the God we are with, has the power and the ability to get rid of everything that will keep us from the life that He wants us to have. He has enough power to get rid of anything. Remember the Lord! He has blessed us in the past, He continues to bless us right the way down to today. Has he not watched over us every moment of our day? Why on earth would we imagine that the God who never changes, who is always faithful, might suddenly walk away and leave us alone today?

God says, "your mouth, your heart, your life, together with my wisdom, my presence and my power, can get through anything." He declares, "we can fix this problem, this giant you face". The Living God declares that it does not matter what we need, He is able to supply it. It does not matter what we face and must overcome, He can do it with us.

When we sit and wonder whether, even with Him we have the strength to make it through the battle we need to recognise the truth that the living God is the almighty God. He is the one who put the stars into space. There is nothing He cannot do. He's a God who made all things, and we have His power within us and are able then to do all He asks of us, through Jesus the Christ who is our strength.

When we wonder whether we have the resources we need. He declares that the cattle on a thousand hills are His. He reminds us, He put the silver in the mine and He put the gold in the earth, He even put the oil buried deep. There is nothing God has promised in His Word which He is not able to do for us. Absolutely nothing.

When we realise we cannot get through things alone but that with Him all things are possible, and we remember He can do all we need, He comes and says, "I will do it, I'm not going anywhere fast. It's not because you're so deserving that I promised to do this. It's just because I am God and I am the God who chooses to love you and the God who chooses to bless you and the God who chooses to be good to you, despite what you were like before I came along." Praise God.

Now if God was like us, He would be changing from day to day. That is why He declares that He is the God who never changes. He says every moment of every day, He just chooses to favour us with His blessing. He comes along and tells us that these are the blessings He can, and will put into our life, if we choose to walk His way, and slay the giants.

There are powerful things that God promises to do, that we may know His favour in our lives day by day. Promises that mean we should be able to see every morning with hope and expectation and come to take to our beds at the close of each day with an awareness of His faithfulness to us and to fulfilling His word and promise.

We need to realise and remember one other thing as we commence this study into the giant nations that seek to keep us from walking in the promises of God and it is something we must always remember in the battle.

I wish that God had said that when we take a giant and slay it, that giant will fall, and that will be a complete end of ever having to fight that particular battle again. But the trouble is, they are not single giants, there is a whole nation of them. The word nation is a word that means there are lots of each wrong attitude and mindset that will come our way.

That is why something like fear comes today, then we overcome it, we rid ourselves of it, and still discover we become frightened all over again the next day. We get rid of one fear, and then suddenly, a month down the road, something happens. We become fearful about something else. Then we wonder why, and are prone to question what is going on. We thought we had dealt with that particular issue in life. No, no, no! Yes we dealt with that giant back there. But there is another one, from the same nation, come to seek to put fear back into our life all over again, to keep us from the promises. It happens.

God says I will get rid of the nation's little by little. Remember the story of David and Goliath. When David came to face the giant Goliath, he walked down to the brook and picked up five smooth stones. He was going out to fight against Goliath. Why pick up five stones? Do you think he was worried he might miss the first time?

Let me tell you why I think he picked up five stones. He had one for Goliath, it would only take one stone, David's aim and God's power would ensure the victory!

David knew that Goliath had four brothers. He took his first stone and slew Goliath. In his heart and mind he said, I am ready for the brothers when they come, I will slay them the same way, with my skill in the hands of the power of the living God. God won a victory that day for his name and for His word. But the four brothers came after David later down the road.

What God is saying to us is this. The minute we slay a giant, we can be excited, but we should not be so excited that we are tempted to think we will never need to face that kind of giant again. Because the giant we slew has got a crowd of brothers. When we deal with the problem of earthly thoughts, God says, "I want you to know the day you get over that earthly thinking, understand, further down the road of your life, another group of similar thoughts are coming your way." The only difference is, the same thing that slew the first one can also hit the others. Providing we are still prepared to pick up the stone, swing and aim the stone, and watch the hand of God take the stone to the right place we will again see the giant fall. When the giant falls, and the bigger they are the harder they fall, when the giant falls, take the sword of the word of God and cut the head off.

So God says we will see Him get rid of the nation of giants, little by little, little by little. 'Little by little' means you can not get rid of them all in one go.

> *And Joshua said to the people of Israel, "Come here and listen to the words of the Lord your God." And Joshua said, "Here is how you shall know that the living God is among you and that he will without fail drive out from before you the Canaanites, the Hittites, the Hivites, the Perizzites, the Girgashites, the Amorites, and the Jebusites." And Joshua said, "hereby you will know that the living God is among you."* Joshua 3:9-10

Do you know that God is with you? We know that He is among us because He says, He will never leave us. He is the one who dwells in the midst of the praise and worship of His people.

But Joshua adds this. He says there is a proof of God's presence. Joshua says there is a way in which we can know that the Spirit of the living God is with us and among us. Joshua says, when the living God is among us something will happen. He will, without fail, drive out from before us the Canaanites, the Hittites, the Hivites, the Perizzites, the Girgashites, the Amorites, and the Jebusites. We ought to underline that phrase, 'without fail'.

That word from Joshua is the only other time all seven nations are mentioned together. The first time is when Moses comes in Deuteronomy and says, "I want you to know that these nations are going to try to keep you from the promises, you have got to destroy them". This second time, Joshua the servant of God declares that we can know that God is among us in this very simple and direct way. God will without fail, bring a giant at a time and give us a way to overcome it. He will without fail, drive them before us and place them under our feet.

Then Joshua lifts the names of the giants before God's people; the giant of low self esteem, of terror, of pride. The spirit of superiority. The giants of destruction, of limited vision, of enjoyment of this world's pleasures, of an unrestrained people and of those who live with no sense of the fear of God in their eyes. Seven nations that want to keep us from the life that God longs for us to have and enjoy, as we walk in His light and His promises.

As we finish this introductory chapter, let us remind ourselves of the words of the Apostle Paul writing to the church in Colossae. Eugene Petersen's Message version paraphrases Paul's words in this way:

> *So if you're serious about living this new resurrection life with Christ, act like it. Pursue the things over which Christ presides. Don't shuffle along, eyes to the ground, absorbed with the things right in front of you. Look up, and be alert to what is going on around Christ—that's where the action is. See things from his perspective. Your old life is dead. Your new life, which is your real life—even though invisible to spectators—is with Christ in God. He is your life. When Christ (your real life, remember) shows up again on this earth, you'll show up, too—the real you, the glorious you. Meanwhile, be content with obscurity,*

> *like Christ. And that means killing off everything connected with that way of death: sexual promiscuity, impurity, lust, doing whatever you feel like whenever you feel like it, and grabbing whatever attracts your fancy. That's a life shaped by things and feelings instead of by God. It's because of this kind of thing that God is about to explode in anger. It wasn't long ago that you were doing all that stuff and not knowing any better. But you know better now, so make sure it's all gone for good: bad temper, irritability, meanness, profanity, dirty talk. Don't lie to one another. You're done with that old life. It's like a filthy set of ill-fitting clothes you've stripped off and put in the fire. Now you're dressed in a new wardrobe. Every item of your new way of life is custom-made by the Creator, with his label on it. All the old fashions are now obsolete. Words like Jewish and non-Jewish, religious and irreligious, insider and outsider, uncivilized and uncouth, slave and free, mean nothing. From now on everyone is defined by Christ, everyone is included in Christ. (MSG)*

Over the next chapters, we will take our time to examine the Scriptures and discover the nature of the Canaanite mind set, the spirit of the Girgashite, what the Jebusite represents, what the Hivites spirit is and what all the other 'ites' refer to in this passage.

I believe we will recognize every one of these giant attitudes as still around in this 21st century. We will recognize them, and take time to realise that the living God has given us the power in His Word and by His Spirit, to take those giants and knock them down, slay them and rid our lives of them, and walk in an abundant life, the life which Jesus the Christ is seeking to give us. We may then begin to walk more fully in the manifestation of the promises of God becoming partakers of the divine nature and escaping the corruption of sin until we all reach the unity of the faith and of the knowledge of the Son of God, to mature manhood, to the measure of the stature of the fullness of Christ, so that we may no longer be children, tossed to and fro by the waves and carried about by every wind of doctrine, by human cunning, and by craftiness in deceitful schemes.

Canaanites

As we began to think about our need to overcome the spirit of the world, we saw in the last chapter that Moses and his successor, Joshua, listed seven nations of giants which stood in the way of God's people, entering into the land of promise. Both Moses and Joshua had been given a promise from God that He would drive out all those nations of giants, as His covenant people moved forward to inhabit the land of promise. But even though God promised to give the people victory they would still have to take responsibility for taking ownership of the land of promise, and be involved in destroying the nations of giants. We also noted the people were to engage in removing the giant nations whilst never entering into conversation with them or making a pact with them.

This commitment from God, to lead His people into a land of promise and blessing driving out all that would keep them from all that He had prepared for them, holds true not only for the people of Israel in Joshua's time, but also for His covenant people throughout the ages. That is to say, this promised commitment is for us also. For every promise in God's word is yea and amen in Christ Jesus, to the glory of God. He has promised to drive out our enemies before us, but has given us a responsibility to be involved by taking action to destroy their influence upon us with the help of the God who dwells within us by His Holy Spirit. These enemies that come against us are bigger and stronger than we are, but with the help of God it is possible to slay them and live day by day in the enjoyment of every promise and which blessing God has declared He will give to His people.

Warring against the abundant life promised by God, and seeking to keep us from the enjoyment of His promises are a host of different elements. They are attitudes, ideas, motives, thoughts, desires, paradigms, all dwelling in the spirit of the age and originating from the lies of the evil one. All seek to keep us from enjoying the life of promise which Jesus came to give to those who would own Him as Saviour and Lord.

The different elements battling us, are described in this portion of scripture as giants. They are bigger, stronger and greater than we can deal with on our own. They seek to come into our life and keep us from knowing and experiencing all that God designed and purposed for us.

These giants battle against us, first of all, to be a snare to keep us from all the blessing that God wants us to have, but they also come against us to turn us off of God. We must be wary and never allow any giant, any thought, any mindset or desire to come into our spirit and make us question whether God is really good, nor must we ever doubt that He is for us, on our side and desiring to reach us, to give us an abundant life, if we are to walk into all the blessing He has prepared and promised to us.

As we look at the nations of giants, remember they are nations. Ridding ourselves of one element, one event, one thought, will not stop the likelihood of another similar one coming against us. Each one can and must be overcome. Our thought patterns can be changed, our habits can be adjusted, our emotions can be harnessed, every thought can be brought into the captivity of Christ. Every pattern of desires can be adjusted. It is possible to learn to love the Lord, our God with all our heart, with all our soul, with all our mind and with all our strength, and to walk into the promises that God has given to His people.

With all that as a reminder we turn to look at the name of the first of those nations of giants.

The lists set out by Moses and Joshua, cover the same seven nations, but they are listed in a different order. Now it may be that the different order is just because those lists were set out by two different servants of God. But I want to suggest that although there is a different order in the names, actually both lists contain a great similarity in significance when it comes to the first of those nations of giants.

In Joshua 3:10 the list starts with the Canaanites. Joshua starts there because the Canaanites were the first of all the other nations. Every other nation of giants flowed from the heritage of the Canaanites. If you follow the line, you'll find that the Canaanite nation came from Ham, the son of Noah. From the children of Ham came all of the other six nations. The significance of the Canaanite as the first nation, is important for us to note.

The attitude, spirit, and mindset, pictured for us in these Canaanite giants, is the origin of all the other issues, attitudes, or mindsets, which will come our way to keep us from walking into God's promises.

If you turn to Deuteronomy 7, Moses lists the nations in a different order. His list places the same significance and impact on the Canaanite nation, but not by listing their name first. Instead Moses draws attention to the Canaanites, as the father of all the other nations, by putting their name as the central nation of giants, then setting three other nations on either side of the Canaanite name.

Sometimes we draw attention to a foundational statement by placing it first, first in importance, first to be considered. Sometimes we draw attention by putting that main statement in the centre and then grouping other elements around it evenly.

I suggest that Joshua lists the Canaanite nation first, as the giant nation of primary importance. Moses puts them in the middle as central in his thinking of the problems we will face. Which ever order we choose to follow as we consider the list of these giant nations, we need to understand this truth that the Canaanite spirit is the most significant and that pretty much every other erroneous attitude and false mindset will flow from the way of thinking represented in this nation. All the other nations are, at root, based around the Canaanite attitude and spirit, and try to come into our life with the same single aim and purpose of spoiling our relationship with, and enjoyment of, God.

When it comes to humanity, God's aim, God's desire, God's longing, God's plan, God's destiny for our lives is to fill them with every promise He has made so we might walk through life under the hand of God, knowing the blessing of God, enjoying an ability to talk with God, and to walk with God, knowing Him as a friend, a good Father, and knowing He will never leave us, and we never need to live in fear, never need to be anxious, never need to be worried, never need to be depressed, never need anything more because we live in the certainty of His blessing, favour and goodness.

That is not to say there will never be times when we experience fears, anxieties, worries, depressing thoughts, or troublesome habits. But every time anything like that happens, we can be sure it is not part of God's design, beyond His desire to help us learn to deal with and remove those thought patterns and attitudes from our lives, making us stronger in our relationship with Him.

We need to learn to always go back to God and remind Him, and us, that He has loved us, and that His love to us is because of His love for His Son. When we became Christian people we were united with Christ Jesus. In Him and through Him, God has made His love known to us, and He has committed Himself to us, as the never changing, ever faithful God. That is the reality we should live with and keep in the forefront of our minds.

The name Canaanite has two meanings in the root of the word. The first meaning of this word Canaanite is 'to bring low'. It speaks of a desire to humiliate and depress. It means to vanquish to the point where rational thinking becomes almost impossible. We will come back to this central thought throughout these chapters. The giants all come to attack the way we think, to try to stop us thinking logically and rationally about life in the light of eternity.

This aim of this first giant nation runs through all of the other six. Everything starts here. It is the fundamental aim of all these giant nations. They seek to depress, to create feelings of humiliation and worthlessness. They seek to vanquish us, and damage our ability to think clearly about life, God, and the gospel of grace and mercy.

All these giant nations come against us to bring us down, lay us low, to remove all hope and expectation of good. They attack the mind, they try to destroy our ability to reason, to think rationally about the fullness of the salvation that has been won for us, and they try to destroy our ability to think in a spiritually real manner.

Their opposition is to the work of the living God. They seek to damage and destroy that work by instilling within us, a mindset at complete odds with Christian thinking. They bring a mindset which is totally contrary to the way of thinking which the Holy Spirit wishes to create and cultivate within us. The triune God comes to lift up, He comes to be a good Father to His children. He comes declaring the value, He finds in people, the love he expends upon them as His own. He comes to make people demonstrations of His ability to renew life and hope.

The giants all come to steal, to kill and to destroy. They come to demolish, to humiliate, to instill feelings of guilt. They come to bring concepts of worthlessness to us, and to convince us we will never have any worth or achieve any lasting value. The giants come and bring a sense of shame to consume hope and joy and make life seem a pointless waste of existence.

That is true of all of these giant nations. It is why we do not sit down and talk to them. It is why we must not try and make an agreement with them. It does not work, we will finish up in doubt and uncertainty. They fill minds with doubt and anxiety. They create uncertainty around the greatest truth known to man, that God thought us of such great value, He sent His only, beloved Son. He gave His Son in order for us to have life in abundance. God did that not because we are so good, so great, so perfect, but just because He chose to love us, He chose to value us, He chose to make us into the jewels of His love, for time and for eternity.

Then the second thought that lies in the root of the name Canaanite comes from what characterised this nation of giants. The word Canaanite speaks of a people who permanently wanted to move around. They never settled. They never stopped moving. They could never find a place of rest, and satisfaction. They were never content. There is no peace to be found in the Canaanite spirit.

Now that should give us a clue that the Canaanite spirit is in opposition to the Spirit of God, for God declares

> *"But the wicked are like the tossing sea; for it cannot be quiet, and its waters toss up mire and dirt. There is no peace," says my God, "for the wicked." Isaiah 57:20-21*

The Canaanite spirit will try to keep us always moving, always trying to find contentment in the next thing, the next moment, the next idea. It comes against us seeking to hinder us from pausing, meditating, becoming still and knowing the living God in the stillness of the present. This

Canaanite spirit is all around us, and quickly finds it's way into our thinking, making us look for the next 'something' to grasp at, as the answer to our contentment.

However, the real revelation in the translation of the word Canaanite is not found merely in the significance of their inability to find rest. The important thought in their constant moving is this. The word Canaanite describes a person who was always moving around with the purpose of buying and selling. They were a nation of merchants and peddlers. They instill a longing to be always moving around in order to acquire new things.

The Canaanite spirit describes this constant desire for the acquisition of things, of more things, of new things, in the hope that the next things which may be acquired would finally bring contentment. They were a people caught up with a material and temporal world. Every day they woke up, they worked out how much stuff they had. They lived with a motivation to discover how to get more stuff. They were always bothered about the quality of the stuff they had, whether the stuff they had worked or not, and what stuff they could get rid of, in order to make room for the next new stuff they were going to get that day. They were never satisfied. All the Canaanite did, and all that drove them day by day and all that kept them going was this driving force and desire always to be getting more stuff.

The Canaanite spirit is all about the acquisition of things, of ever needing, seeking and getting more stuff in the false notion and hope that the stuff they possess can ever satisfy.

Now what is amazing, and what must surely strike us is how relevant this is, and how much it reflects the materialistic world in which we live. This spirit, this attitude could be describing the very way our country and our society exists. This seems to be exactly what the whole advertising world seeks to promote, and all too often doesn't this describe the very thing we do?

Our society encourages us to get stuff. Some of it is essential stuff, some of it is desirable stuff, and some of it is just stuff that we get for the sole reason of getting more stuff. We fill our houses with stuff, and when our houses are full of stuff, we look to get bigger houses because there is no more room left in the place we live to put any more stuff. All to often our minds become consumed with thoughts and worries about our stuff.

We insure our stuff in case we ever lose our stuff. Then if we lose it, we are grateful for the insurance. We claim on the insurance so we can get the same stuff back, and some of that stuff, we have not even used in years.

When I started work after school, I had one suit. It did me. If I needed to dress smart, I could put my one suit on. But as the years have gone on, the number of suits I have, has increased. Some of the suits I have only worn a couple of times, and I look in the wardrobe and am amazed at how many clothes are there, because the truth is, I can only put one set of clothes on at a time.

How many of us have done or seen this. When we come to get dressed, we stand at a wardrobe full of clothes, and say something like this, "I have nothing to wear!" The truth is, we have so much stuff we could wear, we struggle to make a decision on what to wear, and then when we have made the decision, we are anxious about whether it was the right choice, whether it will be the appropriate choice, and we worry, and have all kinds of concerns coming into our hearts and minds in opposition to the peace which God has intended we should know reigning and ruling within us.

Then there are different ways of looking at our stuff. Every thing, every material item we have, all that we have acquired in life, is really just so much stuff. Some of the time we think it is important stuff, but so much of it is actually just stuff we have been persuaded to get, either by the forces at work around us, or by some thought or longing within us which has driven us along.

Whenever we look through magazines, or watch the television, all the time our minds are being bombarded with a blatant attempt to persuade us to gain more stuff. There are so many gadgets, that we are told are essential for life. Yet in truth so often it is just more stuff.

The whole world system, moves us to try and do two things, first to make us think we do not have enough stuff, and then secondly to try to make us set the value on our own life, and on other people's lives, based on the perceived value and amount of the stuff which is owned.

Then, we are encouraged to engage in the world of getting and selling stuff. Have you ever wondered about the auction rooms, and the auction programmes that flood much of our 'entertainment'. They exist on people having stuff they often do not need, stuff they got which they did not really want. Buying stuff that someone does not want and then selling the same stuff to someone else. Often those new purchasers are also people who do not even need the stuff they are buying. They are just collecting more stuff. Then when they have too much stuff they clear out some of the stuff they do not want and sell it on to another collector of stuff.

I talked one day to a lady who clears houses and worked for a local auction room. She was helping me clear my parents bungalow after they had both passed away. As we were clearing the property, I asked her what she actually did for a living. Our conversation went something like this. She said "Oh I can tell you what I do. I go and pick up stuff that nobody wants. I take it back to the auction rooms, and I find people who will buy it." I asked whether the people who bought the stuff really needed the stuff they buy. She said, "All too often no, but they come to the auction because they think they need more stuff and they might get a bargain of something even if they do not really want or need it."

I then asked her to give me an example of the kind of places she goes to pick up the stuff. She told me of a time when she and her husband had gone to clear out a house. It had fifteen rooms. Only one person had ever lived there. She said, they had just finished clearing all the stuff out of those fifteen rooms, and were thinking they had come to the end of the house, when her husband noticed a door which he thought must be out to the garden. He opened the door only to find it led to a passage and an adjacent building with a further six rooms. Every one of those rooms was full of glass items. She explained that her husband and she had looked and wondered how much of this glass had ever been used by the one person living in the house!

The tyranny of the acquisition of stuff is relentless. Now I know that is an extreme example, but let us at least be honest with ourselves. What happens to us in life? All too often we are overtaken with the desire for stuff, we cannot stop thinking about stuff, and we spend our days acquiring more stuff than we will ever need and all too often will not even use. Then at the end of our days, we have to leave all the stuff behind for somebody else to clear and throw away.

Jesus told a story of a man who spent his days acquiring stuff. It is recorded in Luke 12 and from verse 16:

> *And he told them a parable, saying, "The land of a rich man produced plentifully, and he thought to himself, 'What shall I do, for I have nowhere to store my crops?' And he said, 'I will do this: I will tear down my barns and build larger ones, and there I will store all my grain and my goods. And I will say to my soul, "Soul, you have ample goods laid up for many years; relax, eat, drink, be merry."' But God said to him, 'Fool! This night your soul is required of you, and the things you have prepared, whose will they be?'*

There is a further evidence of how far this Canaanite spirit extends into the life we live and the spirit of the world. There was a study carried out looking at the development of language in children. That study discovered that by the time a child reaches the age of two, and begun to speak, the two most common words in their vocabulary are always the same two words. I found this really staggering. The two words they have learned and are the most common in a child's language are identical in any land and in a whole range of different language groups and societal systems.

The first word used most frequently is the word "No". The second most common word used, in every people group is the word that means "Mine".

It suggests that from the very earliest of their days, in all ranges of cultures and languages children are taught and learn first of all to refuse to do what they are asked. Then the second thing they learn is the importance of gathering, owning and keeping hold of their own stuff. They are not old enough to do much, but they have already learned to foster a spirit of rebellion and a spirit of gathering stuff which they hold on to as though it was their own.

That is staggering. Wherever you go around the world, this same attitude is to be found. In every society it is seen to be the same. Whether in almost abject poverty, where little is owned and people live in cardboard shanty areas, or in the richest of societies, the same thing is found. A strength to refuse to do what is asked, and a pride in the stuff they have, mingled with a desire to ensure it is always seen as a personal possession, stuff not meant to be shared, stuff to hang on to, stuff to treasure, stuff to show the value of the owner, because it is stuff owned.
Right the way across the world, it is a sign the Canaanite spirit is alive and kicking. It is this spirit of gathering,

acquiring, wanting, needing, hanging on to, desiring and thinking, all day, every day about stuff. Stuff that somebody else will one day throw away. But valued by me, because it is "Mine."

It starts when we are children. Without the intervention of God and the wisdom and mindset created by the Holy Spirit, it is a mindset which will carry on throughout life, until the day when we leave the stuff behind and realise finally it all had no lasting value and no eternal worth.

One week, I had a couple of hours free, and drove into the countryside around where I was living. I drove down country lanes, just admiring the beauty of the scenery around, and as I drove I found myself on a lane which was a cul de sac. At the end of that lane there was a house. The house was so large I thought it might be a couple of factory units. It was a huge house. There were about twelve windows along the top and twelve windows along the bottom. Then there was a wing jutting out from the back of the building and going off in another direction with a further nine or ten windows. Close to that large building there was a bungalow, and then I noticed between the two buildings, there was a little cottage.

I found a man there, who had come out to see if I was lost and to help me find my way. While we were chatting I asked him who lived in the buildings, only to be told they were occupied just by his wife and him. I wondered whether they moved around from house to house or whether he lived in one and she lived in another, or whether they swap around every so often.

Now I was puzzled, so I asked him what he needed all three buildings for. His answer informed me that they had children and they needed all these buildings to keep and store the stuff their family had acquired over the years.

One of the issues with the Canaanite spirit around the acquisition of stuff is that it will seek to build in our lives the spirit of ownership, the increasing sense of this stuff being 'mine'. It starts by encouraging the desire to gain more, and in the coveting of more things. It then tends towards greed, and works its way onward through a selfish attitude before it finishes up with the belief that stuff is owned and must be held on to by a closed hand.

It stops us thinking sensibly, thinking rationally, thinking spiritually, and with an eye on the eternal. It makes us want to go on and on grabbing and hanging on to more and more material possessions.

There are at least three basic errors within the Canaanite spirit.

The first is the assumption that we own the stuff we have. Then because we think we own it, and it belongs to us and it is ours, we hold it tight in our hands, in case we loose it, or allow it to slip from our grasp. We believe we got it, we will hang on to it, and we will keep it.

The truth is, that all we have, has been given to us by the living God. We think we gained it, by our skill, by our gifts, by our own abilities. Not at all. Even those abilities were given to us by God, and then He enables us to use the gifts and talents He has given to us to gain the things we need in life.

All that I am, He made me
All that I have, He gave me.

It is all given to us in order that we may come and place it back in the hands of the Lord our God. When we offer our material blessings back to Him in service, what we are doing is not really giving back that which is ours, but giving back what He actually just lent to us. We are no more than stewards tasked with looking after the things He has put into our lives, looking after them by using them to bring glory to His name and to the name of our blessed Lord and Saviour Jesus the Christ.

When we start to realise the truth that everything we have is just on loan, for us to use for His glory and to bless others our thinking will begin to move away from the Canaanite mindset the world has sought to teach us and use to mould us, into a Christian mindset. We begin to understand that nothing is ours, it is God's. He has lent it to us, that we might use it for Him.

One of the most lovely things, as our children grow up, is when they come to that stage in life where they want to get us presents maybe for birthdays or for Christmas. It starts, first of all, we buy the present, we wrap it up, we give it to them and tell them to give it back to us at the right time, and we come and say thank you very much. We are trying to teach them something.

But then slowly they reach the stage where they want to get us something themselves, they want to do it to show their love for us, but they do not have the finance to do it.

So they come and ask for some money, which we happily give them, and then they tell us they want it to get something for us. We give them the money, they take what we give them and buy something for us and then bring it back home, wrap it up and give it to us as a gift.

God has given to us. He has poured into our lives, He has blessed us on every side, but His intention was that we would take what He has given to us, and use it in a way that gives glory and honour back to Him. He has blessed us in order that we might bless others. He poured into our lives, not so that we could hang on to what He gives with a tight hand, but that we might hold it in an open palm ready to be used and shared with the world in which He has placed us, that His name might be honoured and praised. Bringing and giving something back to the living God to show how much we love him.

The Christian spirit always looks at what we have and instead of saying "it is mine", it declares that it is all something God has put into trust for us, that we might use it to bless the world and show the living God something of how we feel about him.

The trouble is, we do not want to be stewards. We want to be owners. We want to be people that have all that we have been lent and hold it all for ourselves. We want to hold it in our hands and think of it as our own.

The second thing that is wrong with the Canaanite spirit is that it leads us to judge people based on their stuff. We count their value by how much stuff they have, by what stuff they have. We use their possessions in order to value their existence. That is just crazy.

Have you ever read or seen one of those obituaries which speaks about a person who has died and then says what they were worth. I always want to write and say the person is not worth what they claim, for the value they are counting is not what they have, it is only what they had to leave behind and hold on to no longer. They may have amassed all that stuff at some stage, they might have thought they owned it, but now God has proved to them once and for all they did not own it, it was on loan and it is no longer theirs.

Naked, we came into the world. Naked we have to leave the world. That is why the Lord Jesus told that story about the rich fool. It is also why the Saviour said:

> *Do not lay up for yourselves treasures on earth, where moth and rust destroy and where thieves break in and steal, but lay up for yourselves treasures in heaven, where neither moth nor rust destroys and where thieves do not break in and steal. For where your treasure is, there your heart will be also. Matthew 6:19-21*

We are tempted to count people's value by how much stuff they have and what the quality of their stuff is, but actually our true value is not about how much stuff we have, but what the living God says of us and how much He values us.

God says for every man, woman and child on the face of this earth. "You are so valuable in yourself and of yourself that I gave my only begotten Son." That son, Jesus the

Christ came and died upon a cross, to take away our sin. He did that, not because of the stuff we had. He did it, not because we had something to commend ourselves to God. He did it out of love, out of the worth He put upon us. He reached out in order to save us.

The third basic error of the Canaanite spirit is the belief it creates that the stuff we have is our stuff by right. We have it because we deserve it, and we must look after it ourselves, because we fear nobody else will.

The people that have got a lot of stuff are not necessarily better people than those who have little. In fact very often the more stuff people have, the worse kind of people they become. For the stuff brings a certain tyranny that rules a life.

Have you heard the story of John Paul Getty II. He had so much stuff. In his day he was one of the richest men in the world. He claimed to be all too aware of the duty he had to look after the stuff he owned. He believed it had come to him because he was special. He was so concerned to look after it, in case he lost it by mistake, he had a pay phone installed in his house. When anyone wanted to use the phone, he would point them to the payphone and tell them to use that, even if they were his own family. He thought himself to be something special, some great person, to have acquired all this stuff. Yet like the rest of us, he found he was human, he was not that special, and in the end he left all the stuff he thought he owned behind him. No longer his to possess.

Beware of that Canaanite spirit, it seeks to enslave us with this desire to get all we need, think we need all we can grab, and instills the belief that we must hold on to it all for ourselves, filling ever bigger and bigger barns with all our stuff, building pride within us, until the day we have to let it all go, leave it all behind and find that the only thing we truly needed in life and eternity, has never been gained. Suddenly realising too late, the only thing needful has been missed, and every thing we gained is lost, and now, in eternity, discover even our very life has been lost.

Do not misunderstand me. I have stuff, I have a lot of very nice stuff. God has been very good to me. My lines have fallen in pleasant places. I look at pictures of people around the world and I get staggered by how good God has been to me. I look at pictures of people in this land and I am staggered at how much of the material benefits of this world God has put into my life. In the words of the psalmist He has blessed me in my basket and in my store. But still it is not mine to own. He has lent it to me for a season.

God has been good to me not because I am anything better than anyone else. He has blessed me and been good to me just because He chose to. He did not value me more than another, He just put all this into my life, and one day I must explain before Him how I used the life He gave me and the stuff He lent to me.

I have learned to walk by faith through my life and every month there has been enough to get by. There are some months I still do not know how I got through. Some months I thought I would fail to make ends meet. Then there are some months in my folly, I think, I have done well and managed on my own, and God pulls me up and says He can take it away just as easily as He gave it to me.

There are two verses that have moulded the way I look at stuff, at possessions, at material things, at finances. I keep them before me as a reminder that the stuff I have is not just about the acquisition of stuff. Rather the stuff I have, I have by the goodness and grace of God. I have it in order to use it to bless the world God has put me in.

The first one is in the book of Proverbs. It is one of the texts which has been with me for nearly all my adult life. I learned it first when I went off to Bible College. I was poor in Bible College. I mean, I was really poor in Bible College, I had to have an overdraft just to pay the fees. It was in the days when most students had all their fees paid, but the education authority I came from refused to pay for Bible College training, and the church I belonged to, sent me off to Bible College with a five pound book token and some good wishes.

I did not know in those days, how I would ever manage, and I came across this verse, which became my daily prayer:

> *Remove far from me vanity and lies: give me neither poverty nor riches; feed me with food convenient for me: Lest I be full, and deny thee, and say, Who is the LORD? or lest I be poor, and steal, and take the name of my God in vain.*
> *Proverbs 30:8-9*

I understand there is a spirit in the world that wants me to just keep getting stuff that I do not need. I never want to have so much stuff that I do not know what to do with it. Nor do I want to have so little that I do not know how I will ever get by. God, please make sure that you give me enough, because all things come from you O Lord. All my life He has been faithful to that word.

The other verse which stands against the Canaanite spirit that I want to leave with you at the close of this chapter comes from the New Testament. The apostle Paul in writing to the church in Philippi says:

> *Be careful for nothing; but in every thing by prayer and supplication with thanksgiving let your requests be made known unto God. And the peace of God, which passeth all understanding, shall keep your hearts and minds through Christ Jesus. Philippians 4:6-7*

Then he adds:

> *But I rejoiced in the Lord greatly, that now at the last your care of me hath flourished again; wherein ye were also careful, but ye lacked opportunity. Not that I speak in respect of want: for I have learned, in whatsoever state I am, therewith to be content. I know both how to be abased, and I know how to abound: every where and in all things I am instructed both to be full and to be hungry, both to abound and to suffer need. I can do all things through Christ which strengtheneth me. Philippians 4:10-13*

I want to suggest a different way to live to free us from a Canaanite spirit. When we have a desire in our heart to gain some new stuff, "do I need that?" "Why do I just want to get more? What am I trying to do?"

That is not saying we should live like paupers. Neither is it suggesting we should dress in rags. Certainly there is no justification for us to claim that as Christian people we ought to be poor and have only old and tatty possessions.

That is as much a lie, which denies the goodness of God as the Canaanite spirit which seeks to make us believe we can stand on our own two feet and keep going for more and more and more, yet never finding contentment.

But before we rush to grab the next new thing, and when God places some blessing and favour into our hand let us stop and realize He is doing this for a reason.

When new stuff beckons, let us always recognise that whether we have it or not, it will never be able to make a difference to the contentment we find in life. Let us always recognise and live in the contentment which comes from living every day walking with the living God whose we are, and whom we serve. Let us walk in the contentment of knowing Him, and knowing that all we truly need in life, He has put, and will continue to put into our life and all we desire He alone is able to fulfil. Let us walk in gratitude to Him and hold all the material blessings He gives us in an open palm before Him, ready to use for His glory and praise.

Hittites

As we turn to think about the second nation of giants in Joshua's list, we remember that every one of these nations seek to come against us, to keep us from walking in the enjoyment of the promises God has made within the Scriptures. God desires that we will live in those promises and enjoy the fullness of the destiny He has for us. More than that, God has declared that the clearest evidence of His presence among His people is found in the way they overcome these giant nations and walk instead in the presence and power of the living God.

It is clear, with each one of these nations' names that the giants are still coming to attack us today and that looking at their devices and desires is as relevant in the 21st century as it was in the days of Moses and Joshua. The God who promised to drive out each nation before the people of Israel, still promises to give us victory over them as they come against us today. He does this by placing into our hands all that is necessary to overcome their power, their way of thinking and their attempts to turn us from God. But we must realise the danger and change the way we engage with life in this world, so that instead of being conformed to the ways of this world's thinking, we are transformed as our minds are renewed.

Wherever we turn in the Scriptures and find these nations mentioned, we also discover a problem which follows from their presence; and where they are tolerated as part of the way of life, the problem created is exacerbated and troubles and trials ensue.

In the last chapter we thought about the Canaanites. Each of the other six nations has something of that Canaanite spirit within it. They all want to bring us down and make us think only of this present time, and this material world.

The giant nations not only seek to come against the people of God but they seek to ensure that they govern the world's thinking, and set paradigms for life which the world will follow. As a result we can often find people currently outside of the family of God have their lives affected and governed in a way that brings sorrow and despair upon them. People in the world struggle with these nations of giants. Whole countries struggle with them. Many communities struggle with them. Families experience struggles with them, and even individuals struggle with them. The problem is, the only way to overcome their power to govern the way we think and live is to be found walking in obedience to the ways and power of God.

In this volume we are not really concerned to speak to the way the world may try to deal with the mindset of these giant nations, we are only trying to relate the giant's methods and discover ways to combat them within the life of faith.

Despite that being our main concern, it is worth remembering that many of the lessons we may learn in these pages would also be of help if they were applied to the communities we live among, the nation that we belong to, and even the country and world we dwell in.

The giants are out there, seeking to ensure that nobody

begins to see, believe and walk in the goodness of the mercy and grace of God.

We turn our attention in this chapter to think about the second nation of giants, the nation of the Hittites.

The Hittite giants, and the way they work is certainly as relevant to the 21st century, as it was to the people of Joshua's day, and if the world is still here in another 1000 years, these giants will still be around. That is mainly because Satan has no new tricks, no new methods with which to seek to oppose the work of God and destroy the lives of people. He cannot come up with anything different to try and turn us off from God. There are no new attitudes that he can bring into our life, no new devices that he has, no new desires that he can suggest to us, that he has not already tried in the history of humanity. He still uses the same things, the same lies, the same tricks as he used in the Garden of Eden.

The Hittite giants are one of those ways of working which we will almost instantly recognise and with which we will easily be able to relate, whenever we pick up a newspaper, or turn on a news broadcast. Evidence exists all across the media that the Hittites giants are still plying their skills to create the effects desired by the enemy of souls. Hittite giants are all over the place in the world, in our nation and our communities; and they desire to be all over our families and our individual lives. Day by day, we face Hittite giants.

Understand that names in the Bible are invariably significant. They are not just words that God came up with, or that the people around came up with just for the fun of it. Almost every name is significant. They talk about something, they explain something. All too often we skip over the names because they are hard to pronounce and it seems far too time consuming for us to study out the meaning behind the name.

Even today, everything that we call things, as we use words is incredibly important. The power of our tongue is significant. What we call things matters. If we keep saying to ourselves, we are stupid we are guaranteed to be able to prove our stupidity before long. That is one of the reasons the Bible says 'let the weak say we are strong. Let the poor say we are rich.' We speak truth, and there is power in those words.

The name of this nation is significant. They were not called Hittites by chance. The word Hittite is another of those fascinating Hebrew words. It comes from a root meaning which talks of terror. It tells us that the first thing to understand about this nation of giants is that they seek to create and bring terror. The Hittites are promoters of terror. You could say that the first definition to comprehend when we turn to the Hittites is that these are terrorists. They look for ways and means to create terror and fear.

I guarantee if you pick up a newspaper and look through it, the two things that will strike you as covering most of the pages in that newspaper will have to do with the acquisition of stuff or the creation and effects of terror.

The idea of terror within this word Hittite, is not so much

the idea of a fear which comes from any anxiety which flows from something we are actually experiencing at any moment. There is a fear which comes because of certain experiences we are going through and which can be clearly and rationally explained. For example if we have a bill which needs paying but we do not have the funds to pay it. That may bring anxiety and fear into our lives, but that is not really the kind of fear and terror which comes from a Hittite spirit.

The Hittite terror is based on something which, if only we stopped and thought things through in a rational way, we would be able to allay these fears. Hittite terror speaks of a fear which comes into our minds, into our hearts, into our spirits, and all too often we have no real reason or rational to explain why we are suddenly gripped by fear.

Hittite fear comes and if someone asks us what has suddenly caused this feeling of foreboding, there is very little we can put our finger on and we struggle to find any real rationality for that fear.

Let me give a stupid illustration of irrational fear before we move on to see more of the method of the Hittite giants.

For as long as I can remember, I get terrified, frightened when I see a spider. It does not even need to be a big spider. The very presence of the spider in a room grips me. The moment I see it, everything else goes from my mind, and I am overcome with a completely irrational, illogical fear. Now, when there is no spider there I can ask myself why this happens. After all, spiders are smaller than me, they are unable to hurt me. As a boy, I used to scream, and my mother would come and pick the spider up, carry it away and let it loose. I never stopped to ask how she could do that, I never asked what it was which gripped me with fear. But this kind of terror, is an irrational fear.

That is a silly example, but let me give you some other examples of this irrational terror and fear which comes from the Hittite nation and which is used by this enemy to ruin lives.

Some people are terrified of meeting new people. Some are terrified of being isolated, of being left alone. Some are terrified of being in open spaces. Some are terrified of being in enclosed indoor spaces. Some are terrified of the future, of what might happen tomorrow.

People are terrified of all sorts of things, and really their fears are often totally irrational. Moreover, there is often no obvious reason for the origin of the fear. But their fear brings terror.

Each one of these different terrors has, in these days, been given a name. Most of those names end with the suffix 'phobia' fear, terror. There is even a phobia called 'phobia phobia'. It is the fear of being fearful. Many, if not most of us have times when our lives appear to be governed by some form of irrational terror.

This word terror, speaks of a chill that creeps up upon us, or suddenly stops us in our tracks. It is a Hittite spirit. It's a Hittite thought. It is a Hittite giant, and it is bigger and stronger than we can deal with on our own. It comes to keep us from thinking and calling on the goodness of God. It is all tied up in that word Hittite, for the word speaks of a terror which comes in such a way that it will stop us thinking in a rational way. That is why these fears are so often completely irrational.

They are not merely irrational fears, they are fears which come with the sole purpose and aim of bringing confusion into the mind, to stop us thinking sensibly, or rationally, and above all to stop us thinking spiritually.

Often, just sitting down and talking about the fear and thinking it through sensibly, and logically, brings us to the place where we can recognise and admit the fear we are experiencing is ridiculous.

Even the world understands this. The world has set places where we can go and see some professional person and talk about the crippling nature of our fear. Often these people will advise a course of sessions with a counselor. Now counseling is not necessarily a bad thing, and for many it is a useful, and a valuable means of help.

Counseling for phobias is trying to get people to think through the confusion which the terror has brought and see it as an irrational fear. It aims to make people sit down, talk through their anxieties, face the terror, and take the confusion out of the way in order to bring some rationality to their thinking, to shed light on the confusion, and let that light disperse the terror. What the counsellor is suggesting is that this phobia has brought about confusion in the mind, which has stopped rational thinking. That perfectly describes the meaning of this word 'Hittite'. It is a word, a name which speaks about creating terror, in order to bring confusion to the mind and stop rational and reasonable thought processes.

All too often though, the problem with the world's counseling is that they fail to recognise that this giant of terror is bigger and stronger than any of us. We need the living God to clear the terror out the way and then give us the tools to be rid of it. Only the living God can bring light to bear and when He brings light to the situation, He brings His unfailing wisdom to bear upon the confusion and destroy the fear. For the God we worship is not the God of confusion.

The Apostle Paul writing to the church in Corinth says, I want you to know your God is not the God of confusion, He is a God of peace (1 Corinthians 14:33). In setting that out Paul is drawing attention to the truth that terror and confusion will always rob us of our peace.

The Hittite giant comes to bring terror into our life, to bring confusion to our mind, and stop us thinking, to disturb us, but he is aiming to destroy and remove our sense of peace.

There is one other element behind this name, Hittite, which we need to recognise.

This part of the Hittite name, may best be seen in the story of Goliath. Now I know Goliath was a Philistine. But there is an element in the story of Goliath which casts light on the Hittite giant. Every day Goliath stood and faced the people of God. Every day as he stood on the opposite side of the valley, he shouted out over the people, something like this. "Your God is a crummy God, you ought to have our god, you would be better if you left your God and followed our god". Then the Bible records this:

> *When Saul and all Israel heard these words of the Philistine, they were dismayed and greatly afraid.*
> *1 Samuel 17:11*

That word 'dismayed' is noteworthy for us in this study. It is a translation of a Hebrew word which comes from the same root as the name 'Hittite'. It speaks of demoralizing, and of creating deep depression, of being unable to see any way out of the terror. The word is often translated in the Bible by the word 'discouragement' and 'dismay'. It is a word that speaks of bringing us to the place where we think, we believe, we mean nothing to anybody, and are unable to do anything of any value. We are discouraged. We cannot see any hope for the future, any way forward. We are unable to understand what is happening in our life and we are dismayed, demoralized and depressed.

Now that is the aim of the Hittite giant. He seeks to bring irrational fear, to instill confusion, to stop our minds from thinking, to remove our peace and leave us convinced that there is no hope, no way out of the fear. The Hittites comes to make us depressed and demoralised.

We need to always realise and remember, God never wanted us to live in terror, He never wanted us to have confusion in our minds. God never wanted us to be discouraged or dismayed.

When I was younger I became weary of reading the news which kept suggesting the world would end by being blown up with a nuclear bomb. I got weary of reading of the speculation and concerns around the Cuba crisis, of the Cold War, of the billions spent trying to make sure that if an enemy blew us up, we could blow them up as well. I became weary of reading the speculations and suggestions of coming terror which demanded resources and finances, and all the while the world saw famine and starvation. I became weary of reading it, because it always seemed to bring fear and anxiety into my spirit, around circumstances over which I had no control.

Terror aims to bring confusion, lack of rational thought and then spread discouragement and dismay into individual lives, into family lives, into community lives, into lives of nations and countries, even into the world's life, in order to remove the benefits of peace, the shalom of God, whose purpose in His peace is to change the world for the better.

Both in the book of Joshua and the book of Deuteronomy, when God speaks to Moses about these giants, and when He speaks to Joshua about these giants almost straight away He adds, "Be not afraid, neither be discouraged".

Both the word 'afraid' and 'discouraged' come from the same Hebrew root word which is the origin of this name Hittite. In effect, God says "Do not be affected by the Hittite, do not be affected by the Hittite". "Do not let your courage go from you, do not get to the place where you stop thinking and become confused and dismayed."

God wants us to keep thinking. He gave us a mind so that we could think things through. He gave us the ability to be transformed in our thinking. He gave us the mind of Christ, and the indwelling Holy Spirit to lead us into the thoughts of God.

If you look up the words fear and discouragement in a concordance. you discover, God says more about not being afraid and not being discouraged than he says about almost anything else, outside of knowing him as our own personal, relational, living God. But in terms of what he says to His people, He says more about our need to refuse to allow fear and discouragement into our beings than on anything else.

We were never meant to be terrified. Never meant to be discouraged. We have every reason to be encouraged. We have every reason not to live in terror of anything at all once we are in the care of God.

We should not be discouraged we should not be dismayed, and we should not let terror come upon us because the eternal, unchanging God has bought us to this point. We should ever keep in mind the 'Ebenezer' truth, the "Hitherto" reality. He has kept us and watched over us, up until now.

His love, in time past, forbids me to think
He'll leave me at last in trouble to sink:
Each sweet Ebenezer I have in review
Confirms His good pleasure
to help me quite through.

Begone, unbelief, my Saviour is near,
And for my relief will surely appear;
By prayer let me wrestle, and He will perform;
With Christ in the vessel,
I smile at the storm.   John Newton

Why should we fear? Why should we be discouraged? Why should we be dismayed? If we but look at what He has done for us thus far? He is not a God who is unfaithful. He is not about to cast us off. He is not about to forget us. He is not about to forsake us. Our God is a faithful God. He is faithful in all His ways. He is faithful for all His days. He will not leave us nor forsake us. Why should we ever be discouraged?

There was a time when we thought we were nothing, then the living God came and said, "You were so valuable I sent my Son into the world to save you". The Hittite giant comes to bring dismay and discouragement, to suggest we are worthless. That is just not true. We were worth Jesus's life. How much more could we possibly be worth?

When we are tempted to wonder whether we can ever go on for another day, let us stop and remember, God is not about to change His nature tomorrow? When we are tempted to say that we do not know what is going on in the world, we need to remember whatever is going on in the world, whatever comes our way, whatever happens to us in life, nothing can separate us from the love of God in Christ Jesus. If we die, we find ourselves in glory. If we don't die, His grace is sufficient to carry us through. He who brought us this far will never leave us.

I love the prayer of Hannah in 1 Samuel 2.

> *"My heart exults in the Lord; my horn is exalted in the Lord. My mouth derides my enemies, because I rejoice in your salvation. There is none holy like the Lord: for there is none besides you; there is no rock like our God. Talk no more so very proudly, let not arrogance come from your mouth; for the Lord is a God of knowledge, and by him actions are weighed. The bows of the mighty are broken, but the feeble bind on strength. Those who were full have hired themselves out for bread, but those who were hungry have ceased to hunger. The barren has borne seven, but she who has many children is forlorn. The Lord kills and brings to life; he brings down to Sheol and raises up. The Lord makes poor and makes rich; he brings low and he exalts. He raises up the poor from the dust; he lifts the needy from the ash heap to make them sit with princes and inherit a seat of honor. For the pillars of the earth are the Lord's, and on them he has set the world. He will guard the feet of his faithful ones, but the wicked shall be cut off in darkness, for not by might shall a man prevail. The adversaries of the Lord shall be broken to pieces; against them he will thunder in heaven. The Lord will judge the ends of the earth; he will give strength to his king."*

That is the way to kill Hittite giants. Hannah comes in praise and says her heart rejoices in the Lord. Her heart is exalted in the Lord. What she is saying is, that her heart is just remembering God. She was afraid, but she just remembered God, and as she remembered Him she found herself rejoicing in the salvation He had brought her.

Then she comes and tells anyone who will hear or read her song that she wants them to know, there is nobody holy like the Lord, for there is none beside him. Who is a rock, like God, there is nobody else we can depend on. Nobody else will stick with us like the living God. Nobody else will stay beside us and hold us up, like the living God.

Look at what she says, "Do not talk to me proudly. Do not let arrogance come out of your mouth. Because the Lord is a God of knowledge. He lifts up. He casts down. He makes poor, He makes rich. He goes to the poor who are in the dust and He lifts them up. He goes to those who think they do not need God and He puts them down. All this He does according to his own purposes. The Lord kills and the Lord makes alive."

Her whole attitude of heart and life is summed up in this thought. When we are walking with the living God, rejoicing in God, we can be certain that whatever comes our way, nothing can destroy us unless God allows it. We are still breathing because God allows it. We are still standing because God enables us to. He has not let us down. He gives us the air we need to breathe. Let us get that into our hearts and minds.

I used to travel around the world a little bit. Often I would be asked whether I felt safe? I would always board the aircraft and in my heart I would say to God "well here I go either the scheduled destination or glory." It did not matter which would be my arrival point, the advertised destination or the immediate presence of God, all was in the hand of the God who loved and cared for me.

Then Hannah continues "The Lord alone is the one that puts down and picks up. He picked me up and you know what? He raises up the poor out of the dust, He lifts up the beggar from the dunghill." She declares that God has said that when people had nothing, and when people had no hope, He alone is the God who lifts us up. When He picks us up He makes us a royal child, and causes us to inherit the throne of his glory.

Every terror that comes towards us, and every fear that comes against us, comes to stop us thinking, stop us remembering, stop us seeing the wonder of what God has done and what He has promised. The terror comes to bring confusion and discouragement into life and stop us realising that God has picked us up, He has set us on high, He will cause us to inherit the throne of his glory, and nothing and nobody can stop it, for they have neither sufficient power or ability to stop God doing all He has said, or to make Him change His mind.

God is the one who gives us life. He is the one who says when our days are ended. He is the one who alone is able to lift up. He alone is the one who is able to bring down. He is the one who is able to keep our steps so that none can make us slip. He is the one who lifts up the poor and causes them to inherit His throne. He is the one who will destroy the confusion, and bring clarity.

The Apostle Paul, writing to the church in Corinth says we need to know and understand something important about our minds. When we start to think things, when we start to imagine things, when we start to wonder things, we should take all of those thoughts, every one of our imaginations, with those doubts and wonderings and bring them into the captivity of the obedience of Christ. Remembering the Lord your God.

> *Casting down imaginations, and every high thing that exalteth itself against the knowledge of God, and bringing into captivity every thought to the obedience of Christ. 2 Corinthians 10:5*

Every day the Saviour walked upon the face of the earth, He walked in communion with His Father. Whatever came His way, He walked in communion with His Father. He was obedient, every step of the way to what His Father required. See that obedience of Christ to everything that came His way and how He walked with His Father. When Judas came to betray Him, He walked in obedience to His Father. When Peter came to try and turn Him away from going to Calvary, He walked in obedience to His Father. The Apostle says we should look at that obedience and realise He never faced a moment on His own.

Paul then goes on to say that as we look at the Saviour's obedience we should learn to live the same way. When a thought of terror comes, when it first seeks to enter our minds, even when it first tries to come in to our life through our eyes or via our ears, we must learn to run to God, and as we run to God, ask ourselves why should we fear when the living God is ours.

> *Who shall separate us from the love of Christ? Shall tribulation, or distress, or persecution, or*

> *famine, or nakedness, or danger, or sword? As it is written, "For your sake we are being killed all the day long; we are regarded as sheep to be slaughtered." No, in all these things we are more than conquerors through him who loved us. For I am sure that neither death nor life, nor angels nor rulers, nor things present nor things to come, nor powers, nor height nor depth, nor anything else in all creation, will be able to separate us from the love of God in Christ Jesus our Lord. Romans 8:35-39*

It is why as the Saviour came to his last words, just before leaving His disciples, knowing that terrorism, terrorists, terrors, fear, and confusion, were going to come against them, He declared, 'Lo I am with you always'. Do not be afraid. I am with you even to the end of the ages.

The Hittite giants come because Satan is after our minds. He is after our minds to bring terror and confusion, deep discouragement and dismay. We must learn to tell him, he has no right to our minds, and instead of letting him bring terrors to us, we must show him that we are those who take every thought into the presence of God. Every day, we will remember that He who brought us safe thus far, is able to carry us through to the throne of His glory.

The God of heaven will help us keep fear from our minds, as we bring our thoughts and imaginations under His control.

> *You keep him in perfect peace whose mind is stayed on you, because he trusts in you. Isaiah 26:3*

It is no surprise the Hebrew word used and translated as

'mind' in this verse, is the word that speaks of the imaginations of the heart and mind. It speaks of the creative imaginations that come from our being.

The prophet says, perfect peace is assured to those who keep the mind, the imagination, the creative thoughts that come from our being all leaning on the person and power of the living God. For the Hittite fear will find no way to molest or trouble those who have learned to lean on the everlasting arms of that God, and depend upon Him who has promised to keep us, .

When fear comes, resist the Hittite giant, remember the Lord who promises to drive this giant also away.

> *And let the peace of Christ rule in your hearts, to which indeed you were called in one body. And be thankful.Colossians 3:15.*

Hivites

We turn next to think about the third nation of giants listed by Joshua, which he claims God has promised to drive out before us. The victory we have over these nations of giants is the evidence of the presence of that living God among us. This third nation of giants is the Hivite people.

Moses tells us that all seven of these nations were giants. He uses the word giant as an indication that these nations will come against us with a power and force which we will never manage to overcome on our own. They come with a spirit, an attitude, a thought process which is opposed to the way and will of God, and their craft and technique will overcome us, unless we stand against them in the power of the risen Christ.

When we come to this third nation of giants, there is a similarity between this nation and next. The name Hivite comes from the same root as the word Perizzite, the name of the fourth nation. So there is some similarity between these two nations. Therefore, some of what we discover relating to this third name will have a bearing on the fourth name. The word Hivite and the word Perizzite both come from a Hebrew root word which speaks of village dwellers.

We need to be very careful here because this is not intended to be seen just as a word spoken against the literal dwelling places of anybody who happens to live within a village setting. It is not saying we should all be town dwellers. We need to think more carefully than that.

Yet there can be some characteristics of people who lived in villages, especially in days gone by, which God is wanting us to think about and learn from. There are village mindsets that we need to understand.

Most village dwellers these days, are aware of more than the village they live in, and many of those who now live in villages have not always lived in the same place. That was not always the norm. In Bible times it was more common to find that those who lived somewhere, had always lived in that location. We need to remember that as we come to think about these two nations of village dwellers.

The other thing we need to recognise is that whilst the root word behind the name Hivite and Perizzite is the same word, there are significant differences in the developing of that root into the two different names of these nations. While there are some similarities, these two nations are not coming with identical issues and thought patterns with which to attack us. Both names speak of village dwellers, but each one has a slightly different angle on what it means to be a village dweller.

The word 'village' means something specific in the scriptures which set the village apart from the towns and cities. We will discover that the Perizzite name concerns some of those specifics of villages and village dwellers in Bible times. But the word for village dwellers in the name for Hivites represents a different attitude of heart. The idea of village dweller in the Hivite name represents and demonstrates a way of thinking that many of us who have been around church for a long time will readily recognize.

To understand the issue the Hivite represents we need to remember that today, in the UK, we live in a very mobile society. People move home, and they tend to travel widely. It was not like that in Bible times. Indeed, it was not like that in this country in the past. We only need to look back a few decades, maybe to the early part of the last century, and you could find people who were born in a village, lived in a village, went to school in the village, worked in the village and died in the same village, never moving beyond the confines of their village.

That way of living easily fostered an attitude which led to villagers imagining that the only thing of significance was their own life in their own village. It tended to foster a way of thinking which suggested the whole world revolved around the village, as though there was nowhere else with either importance or significance beyond that small local environment.

It may seem difficult to comprehend how it was possible to live like that, especially now with the advances in technology which are making the other side of the world seem so very close. We can find it difficult to imagine ever living with the thought that the only thing which exists and matters on this planet, is the life we live, in the house we call home, and the road we live on. We all know that such a view is just simply untrue.

Yet, for all that, some of the spirit flowing from that introspective, small minded and self centred mindset can still quickly enter our hearts and lives. It is a mindset that thinks in village terms, that considers things only in terms of a small, local, scenario and makes self the centre of everything we think, plan and do.

In the Hivite mindset the whole paradigm of life has to do with our own little world. The attitudes it manifests flow from an overwhelming sense of the importance of our own small circle of life and thought. It encourages limited thinking, it prefers small, all of it's thoughts are small, and it only ever desires to comprehend a small vision. If a person with a Hivite mindset hears about anything big, they will seek to find a way to reject the idea, or the thinking behind it. Any other response they find too uncomfortable to consider.

They fear anything that will challenge their own local, small mindset. They worry that if their world ever changed from being small, it would change the whole character of their world to an unrecognisable and unfamiliar concept outside of their comfort zone. They want to stay with the familiar, the comfortable, the inward looking, self serving mindset that has been their trademark.

They are recognised by the smallness of their vision, the limited ideas which they will ever allow to engage with their thought processes and the confined nature of their attitudes.

We need to understand that the Hivite concept of small is not necessarily intended to be a numerical postulation. Indeed you can have a village of a few thousand. The numerical size is not the issue. Small, in the Hivite sense is more concerned with an inward focus where everything is familiar, with no thought of the possibility for change or challenge.

It speaks of those with no thought for anything or anyone outside of their immediate circle. It results in a mindset which, before long, leads to a small and petty way of thinking and acting, while believing that there is nothing worthwhile beyond their current circle of little ideas and restricted ways.

One area which can reveal this small mindedness, is a desire to fight over issues which nobody else is really concerned about, to hold on to every element of thought which they possess, never allowing any new concept, or truth to be considered for fear of undermining the whole structure of their life thinking.

Something significant and recognisable flows from that kind of tiny, petty way of thinking which inhabits the Hivite people, these village dwellers.

There are three places we are told about in Joshua 9 where the Hivites lived. Whether that was the total extent of that nation or not is less certain. Yet from those three locations and accounts we can see and discover that this nation was prepared to do anything to maintain their status quo, and their comfortable way of living.

They are characterised by this desire to maintain things as they are, to keep everything the same. They live with a maintenance mentality. They desire to keep everything exactly the same for the rest of their days. They think nothing should ever change.

Now I have some sympathy with that, because change is always difficult, and we live in a world where change is coming at us so very quickly. It is coming at the speed of life. There was a study done which suggested that we will see as much change in our lifetimes as the world saw over the previous five hundred years, and that rate of change is only accelerating.

But the Hivite says "I do not want to change and I will do anything in order to avoid change so that I can maintain what I know, and hold on to what is comfortable". In this way they live with their small and often petty ways. One of their favourite phrases is: "It is not like it was years ago". It is a Hivite spirit.

They start with a small attitude, and a limited vision. They move on to being petty, and then proceed to adopt a maintenance mode. Before long they are irrelevant, left behind in a world that has moved on. More than that, they loose sight of the living God, who is always moving forward. We never want to find ourselves staying where God used to be!

I saw this definition of village dwellers in the Reader's Digest Dictionary. It said: "Village dwellers are people who are happy with their small community, and want to ensure that nothing changes or threatens this small group, they are people who keep themselves in their own quaint and peculiar ways."

It is the Hivite spirit which lives with this desire to hang on to the familiar, even where others may see it as quaint and peculiar. Unwilling to change, unwilling to move, unwilling to dream of something better, unwilling to consider anything or anyone beyond themselves. They like small, quaint, and odd, they are unwilling to do anything, to change anything, because they are convinced, they have to maintain their small little ideas, and their inwardly focused little group.

There was a time when my father was president of the Southern Baptist Association (SBA). As president of that Association, he had the chance to travel around preaching in all of the churches within the group. It was a great opportunity for him, and one which he was always grateful to have been given. But, he told the story of going one day to a church which was known as a rural and tiny place. When he arrived he walked in and found they had advertised that the president of the SBA was coming to minister and amazingly a good number of visitors had turned up. At the close of the service, he went to meet people as they left the building. As one elderly person was leaving my father asked whether it was her church. She intimated that it was. He then expressed the view that it must have been lovely for her to see the building with so many people in for the service only to find she responded to this comment by saying, "Well, I don't know, we like it best when it's only we."

It is a Hivite mentality. Only thinking small. Never wanting to expand their view of things, of God, of the world, of the work of God, of the spread of the gospel. Petty, narrow, not willing to change. Always desiring to keep within their own group and comfort zone.

God's method of working, throughout the whole of the Bible, has been to bless His people. He has done this with the revealed purpose that those who have been blessed by Him are blessed in order for them to become the channel of blessing for others. He blessed Abraham, in order to bless the world. He blessed the Israelites, His own special people, and set out His purpose for them to go and teach the world about God and establish the worship of the one and only true God.

The whole mentality of doing anything, just for the good of our own selves, or our own family, or our own fellowship is an anathema to the plan and purpose of God. He set in place a gospel and gave a commission with a world view, a command to go into all the world to meet the world, and to change the world for the better. God has never been a part of any small, petty, inward looking mentality.

With all that said and the clear evidence of the scripture on this outward looking desire of God to bless the world, we still seem all too often to meet people who devote their time and energy to maintaining their position, so nervous of any activity diluting their interpretation and understanding of issues, that they refrain from ever engaging with anyone or anything who may hold ideas and views different to them. As a result they never fulfil the purposes of the God who blessed them in order that the blessing He gave them would be shared with others who need to know Him, and experience His favour towards mankind.

There is another attitude hidden away in the root of this name Hivite. The first focus is on the idea of village dwellers, but there is a second focus in the meaning of the root of this name. It flows from this opposition to change and the fear of what change might do to them. There is within the Hivite nature, the tendency always to being negative about everything.

Whenever change is suggested, whatever idea is proposed to move things forward, the Hivite will find a reason why it should not be tried.

We can spot the Hivite spirit rising within us whenever we are tempted to suggest either of these responses. 'The new idea has been tried before and it did not work last time so there should be no change now'. That really is an interesting argument, which if followed through in every area of life would leave the world in a very strange place with none of the advances which have been made over time.

On the other hand, if the proposal for change and growth has not been tried before the Hivite will come with a statement along these lines; 'This has never been done that way before, so it really should not be tried now.'

Both of those statements are normally aligned with a theological argument that no matter how much the world has changed, the spiritual condition is the same as it always has been, and God does not change. Well, that is certainly true, and yet God has moved on from the days of the types and shadows of the Old Testament, and even if you read the book of the Acts of the Apostles, you find the methods and means of sharing the eternal truths of God changed from place to place and over the time span of those early years.

It really does not seem to matter what new method or means are suggested, a Hivite will always have a reason for not moving, for not changing, for not trying something, for not looking beyond the needs and comfort of the current circle.

That negativity really comes from this unwillingness to change. They like it the way it is. They enjoy the comfort of familiarity. They like their own setting, their own community, their own little group. Every time you hear that kind of negativity, remember, it is not supposed to be the Hivites church, it is meant to be the church of the living God. It is the church that Jesus Christ said He would build, and it is the church that Jesus Christ said would turn the world upside down.

We are supposed to impact, challenge and change the world. Our aim as christian people is to win the whole world to the living God. Jesus Christ took eleven people and said, "Go into all the world." He never said "stay in your little group". The Saviour has a picture of, and a passion for, the whole of humanity, lost in its sins, lost in its deadness, lost in its despair, lost in its misery, lost in its degradation, lost in its total waywardness.

But the Hivite is negative. Everything suggested will find a negative response. Hivites raise concerns about the danger of change, the dangers of leaving tradition and moving outside the security of their own familiar circle.

One of their favourite responses, intended to warn of the dangers of looking beyond themselves are found in phrases like this; "It will change the way we are." As though that would always be a bad thing. Or these "it wasn't like this in the old days"; "We won't be the same." The problem is, God never intended us to stay the same!

Do you remember what is was like when you would go to a church and they used a kind of subculture language? When everyone spoke using "Thee and Thou", and a whole range of language from years ago, speaking in 16th century english and adding long theological words, without explanation, where few people, if any, really understood the meaning of the words.

Village dwellers, wanting to stay small, wanting to stay odd, wanting to just hang on to things and keep their narrow, petty ways. Not understanding that the nature and love of the God we worship is not only a mile deep, it is also a mile wide.

You can find Hivites refusing to recognise that the God who meets with His own in one fellowship of people may just be the same God who is meeting with another, different group of Christians in a church down the road.

Every time you come across that kind of attitude know that God says, He will drive out that Hivite spirit, that Hivite giant, that Hivite nation. But if you do not put that way of thinking to death, it will keep coming back. It keeps wanting to invade our walk with God to keep us from moving forward with God, to make us avoid stepping out of our comfort zone, hanging on to, and defending theological niceties that are insignificant to a lost and dying world.

One of the great dangers of developing a Hivite spirit is seen in a desire to remain the same, remaining where God used to be, trying to work with the things God used to empower, not realising He is the God of new things, and new ways.

While God is never changing in Himself, and the wonder of the gospel message remains eternally constant, the method, the style, the options of how that unchanging message is brought to the world is always changing.

Allowing a Hivite mindset to come into our thinking will leave us as village dwellers, full of negativity, small minded, petty, hanging on to where God used to be and how God used to work.

But there is an even graver danger we must be wary of if we find our way of thinking being affected by the mindset which this giant desires to instill within us.

The conviction of holding on to all we know and never changing anything, can instill a view that we are like this because we are right. That slowly breeds a kind of self righteous conviction, that we are the only ones who really know the truth and are unprepared to compromise or challenge anything. We can become so convinced of our rightness that we believe we have a monopoly on the truth and on the being of God.

That is a dangerous place to be. It empowers self

righteousness, and strengthens a pharisaical attitude. It fosters an unwillingness to hear God say anything apart from what we already know. Whereas God intends for us to all be seekers, pursuers, followers, and learners of the truth. We look to Him to speak new things into our lives. We look to Him to change us, to grow us, to move us. Because healthy things grow, and growing things change. Changing things challenge and challenge forces us to trust God. Trust leads to obedience, obedience makes us healthy, and healthy things grow. So the circle of the activity of God in our lives continues until we see Him face to face.

There was a day when I was grateful that churches looked as though nothing had changed for the last 100 years. There was a day when I thought that was right. There was a day when I did not like musical instruments in church. There was a day when I had sympathy with those who believed the organ was the devil's own instrument. Then as I began to read the scripture and look for God to speak to me, God began to open my vision to realize new things about Himself. To discover new truths about the living God and His worship, and I slowly I began to seek to slay that Hivite spirit within me.

I began to discover that God was able to speak to people with a different tradition and churchmanship to me. Then slowly over the years, I began to realize that God was able to reach other people as well as those I felt He should be able to reach. I even discovered He met with people I had thought He ought not to meet with. Slowly I moved from a kind of self righteous fool into a way of realizing that God is a great God. He is a big God. God was not just in my little tribe, in my little group, in my little way. God was working all over the world, in a range of church traditions and a host of worship styles among a plethora of different people.

I began to see the externals of worship and fellowship were almost insignificant to God, as long as the central message of the gospel of saving grace was maintained. The message never changes, but the methods we use are just ways to get that message to a lost world. I discovered for myself the truth written in an old hymn.

The love of God is broader
Than the measure of man's mind,
And the heart of the eternal
Is most infinitely kind. Frederick Williams Faber

I knew a man who went to became the minister in a village church. He and I came from the same kind of background and churchmanship. He went to minister in this church and on arriving there found he had a congregation of about twenty people. After he had been there for some years, the congregation had reduced to five people. In time the congregation had reduced further until only three remained; him, his wife and the organist. I remember talking to him and asking how he saw things in his ministry. He told me that God was purifying the church. He still was not sure whether the organist was truly saved, but he thought that at least his wife was. I discovered later that whenever one of the congregation questioned whether he was right about anything, a disciplinary meeting was held and they were put out of the fellowship. May God preserve us from such who claim to represent the living God who loves the world.

When he gets to glory, if he is truly a follower of Jesus Christ, I think he will have a shock coming. Arriving there, he will discover that he did not know everything, and actually the only ground for entry is to have believed on the Lord Jesus Christ, to have opened the heart to Him, and been cleansed from sin in that precious blood which flowed from Calvary.

The Hivite way of thinking, with this idea that the smaller we are, the more blessed and the more pure we have become is just so wrong. It is found nowhere in the Bible.

Overcoming a Hivite spirit has been a battle for me. There are some things we need to ensure we do, in order to rid ourselves of this particular nation of giants.

Always look for the good. Always look for positive signs of God at work. Always be open to God and keep our view of God big. Never withdraw from a promise that God has given to us because we think it is too big for us to see fulfilled. Always give glory to God. Always be fully persuaded that what God has said, He is able to perform.

When we read the story of Abraham, we discover that Abraham was old when God came and reminded him of the promise made years before. God told Abraham when he was one hundred years old, that the time was drawing near to fulfil the promise of a child, a son and an heir. Abraham came and told his wife, who was then about ninety, that she was about to bear a child. Sarah thought he had to be joking.

Now let us be honest, at ninety the idea that she would

give birth, and then wean a child on breast milk, and that at a hundred Abraham was going to father a child really does all sound impossible. Actually when Abraham told Sarah what was going to happen, the Bible says she replied and told him it could not happen because from her side nothing was working anymore. Actually she said it appeared from her perspective that his body was not working either. So she is recorded as saying something like; "Abraham, none of it's working. You're not working. I'm not working. So you have just got to be joking". Abraham's reply was the response of faith. He declared that whether it seems possible in the natural or not, he had a promise that God was going to do this for him. He might be a hundred, but he declared that he knew the son would arrive within the next nine months or so, because of that promise from God.

That kind of attitude will kill off a Hivite spirit. Learn to recognise the promise of God, and then hold fast to that promise, whatever the circumstances. Whatever anyone else says, however things may appear, the promise of God is the one and only true reality. We need to live day by day with a determination to walk in that word from God until He fulfils it. He has never yet failed to do all He has said.

The Apostle Paul writing about Abraham's situation said "he fainted not". "He staggered not." The word translated fainted or staggered is a word which means he let nothing in his mind which would lay aside the truth of the promise.

Everyone else was telling him that he ought to realize God

could not do what Abraham claimed he had been promised. Everyone was telling him he was past it. Even his own physical body declared to him, he was past it. Abraham refused to stagger. Instead he kept saying, "I might not see it yet, but I'm still going to speak it, and as I speak it, God's going to bring it into being."

That is what faith does. Faith continues to speak and believe the promise of God, until God brings His word into being.

It is the way to overcome the Hivite spirit, instead of speaking to the Hivite giants, believe in the promises of God. Exercise strong faith. Take the promise and claim it for ourselves. Believe the promise, and learn to start to speak the promise, declaring the promise, and believing God will bring His word to pass, to fulfil all that He has ever said. As people come and tell us that it will never happen, that things cannot change, or that we will never grow, we ignore them and begin to speak positively about what God has said and what He can do. God has said, He will drive out the Hivite, He will drive them out before us, and our strong faith will slay the Hivite spirit and remove it far from us.

One last thing. If you read into Joshua 9, you find that Joshua made pacts with no nations at all, except for the Hivites.

The Hivites came along lied and pretended that they were not really Hivites. They suggested they were not really small minded village dwellers. They told Joshua, they had travelled a long way and just wanted to be safe and live among the people of God. They told him they were keen to be with him and be part of what he was doing. Joshua, let them in. He let them in just after the Israelites had won the victory at Jericho. He was tricked, and made a pact with this group of Hivites.

Year after year, the nation of Israel struggled after that, because every time Joshua said "let us go and do this", there were people in their midst who opposed the suggested move, on the basis of a perceived impossibility of doing anything to move forward. The Hivites are like all the giant nations. We dare not make a pact with them. We dare not let them have any part of our thinking. We must hold tight to the reality, God is a big God and has given unto us 'exceeding great and precious promises by which we may walk'.

If ever we hear anybody suggest that the promise of God is not for us. Thank them, by all means, but move from them and from their thinking. Never allow that negative spirit to come close. Move on from them and walk on into the promise. They will try to make an agreement with us, to help us, but understand that all they really want to do, is what every one of these giant nations want to do. They desire to bring negativity and doubt into our minds in order to turn us off of God.

They want to bring doubts to keep us from receiving what God has promised for us. They want to keep us from growing and changing, to stifle our life in God. We must not allow them to do it. God's people were never meant to be small, petty, negative, with a maintenance mentality. God is not like that, everything He does changes as it grows with life, vitality and power.

Even when the prophet quotes God as saying "He stretched the heavens" he uses a term which means God is still stretching them, increasing, enlarging, growing and changing them. God wants to do the same in our lives both individually and corporately. He wants to stretch us, enlarge our hearts, grow our faith, and change us into the people He designed us to be, fully reflecting His glory and the beauty of our Saviour.

Keep away from the Hivite spirit and walk in faith, in the promises of God, with the life of God within you.

Perizzites

We turn next to think about the Perizzite giants. In the last chapter, we noted that the name Perizzite comes from the same root word as Hivite. Both come from a Hebrew word refering to village dwellers. But when you come to this word Perizzite there is a very specific thought behind the meaning of the word which describes this kind of village dweller.

In the 21st Century we live in what is often referred to as a 'global village'. That concept gives some significance to the difference between the parochial village dweller described by the word Hivite and this second group, the Perizzites. The Perizzites also lived in villages, but this word does not refer to the insular nature of village life. It has more to do with a concept of village within the biblical meaning of the community of dwellings described as 'villages' as compared to those communities which made up 'towns' or 'cities'.

In Bible times the major distinguishing feature which separated a village from a town was not the size of the population, nor the delineation of the area inhabited. A town or a city was called by that name by virtue of a wall which surrounded the area where people dwelt. That boundary wall turned the habitation from a village into a town or a city. The significant, and only real difference then, between towns and villages was found in this fact that the term village referred to a community living in an open space, an area without walls, or boundaries, enclosing that space.

Village dwellers, lived in open unbounded areas. They lived without boundary markers to show where the edge of the village was. If they ever erected any kind of boundary marker it was done in a way where the marker could be easily moved whenever the inhabitants saw a need to adjust the confines of the village.

It may be that in some respects the Perizzite mindset can appear similar to the Hivite, but in most ways the Perizzite mindset is almost a complete opposite, for it denotes a person who delights to live without boundaries. They choose to live with no limits, and even the parameters they have are easily moved to suit changing moods, passions and times.

The Perizzite spirit seeks to live without any fixed boundaries and rules. Even the limitations they acknowledge are moveable fixtures and adjustable rules depending on any change of condition or circumstance.

When we thought of the Hivites we saw their way of being village dwellers led them to be small minded, restricted, petty, with a desire to keep doing things in the same way things had always been done. The Perizzite as a village dweller is almost diametrically opposed to that mindset. The dangers to be found in this Perizzite attitude needs to sound a warning note whenever we seek to kill the Hivite mindset within us.

In determining to avoid the Hivite mindset, and seeking to make a concerted effort to be open to change, and avoid always seeking to ensure everything remains the same, we face the temptation to go to the other extreme and think there are no fixed boundaries, no lines which cannot be crossed in what we think, what we desire and what we do. All too quickly we can find ourselves in a place where we think we can only be happy with things that are always different. It can create a mindset of always looking for some new idea, some new thing. It opens us up to becoming like the Athenians 'always looking for some new thing' (Acts 17:21). We can be tempted to think that the way to move with God is to always be looking for what is new and always moving away from anything that may have been done before.

Let us start with that danger flowing from the Perizzite mindset, and take a couple of examples of where that way of thinking can lead us.

There are some people who believe we should not engage in singing a song, if it was written any earlier than last year. Certainly there are also some who will not countenance singing anything written after the mid 1900's, and that has to be wrong, but the idea that we should not sing anything which was written more than 20 years ago, has to be just as wrong. It throws out good material in an attempt to be always seeking new things.

The desire not to be stuck where God is not, and to keep being relevant to the age in which we are found, all too easily leaves us in danger of undermining the very foundations of our faith.

Years ago, I used to recite a poem called the new duckling. It contains deep truth about the dangers of the Perizzite desire to always want to be new and do new things.

"I want to be new," said the duckling.
"O, ho!" said the wise old owl,
While the guinea-hen cluttered off chuckling
To tell all the rest of the fowl.

"I should like a more elegant figure,"
That child of a duck went on.
"I should like to grow bigger and bigger,
Until I could swallow a swan.

"I won't be the bond slave of habit,
I won't have these webs on my toes.
I want to run round like a rabbit,
A rabbit as red as a rose.

"I don't want to waddle like mother,
Or quack like my silly old dad.
I want to be utterly other,
And frightfully modern and mad."

"Do you know," said the turkey, "you're quacking!
There's a fox creeping up thro' the rye;
And, if you're not utterly lacking,
You'll make for that duck-pond. Good-bye!"

"I won't," said the duckling. "I'll lift him
A beautiful song, like a sheep;
And when I have - as it were - biffed him,
I'll give him my feathers to keep."

Now the curious end of this fable,
So far as the rest ascertained,

Though they searched from the barn to the stable,
Was that only his feathers remained.

So he wasn't the bond slave of habit,
And he didn't have webs on his toes;
And perhaps he runs round like a rabbit,
A rabbit as red as a rose. *Alfred Noyes*

Some things change, some things will never change, some things need to be made anew, some things must be kept as they always have been. The idea of always having to throw things out just because they have been done that way before is wrong. It cannot be right to say that every tradition must automatically be wrong, just because it is a tradition. That way of thinking will leave us permanently looking to do things that are new. It will leave us feeling that anything done before, must not be done again. That mindset promotes always being new, different, modern, unique. The latest idea, and thinking is a mantra all to likely to leave us with nothing in our lives and service for God, but worthless feathers, without any real lasting substance.

When the Apostle Paul came to Athens, he said the Athenians were a people who spend all their time trying to discover some new thing. They epitomised this Perizzite spirit. They wanted to live in a way that threw over all the traces, all the restraints, all the things that had ever been done before, in order to be frightfully modern.

We must be open to make some changes, certainly. We need to be aware of the times we are living in, that is true. We should also ensure that we stay real and relevant, absolutely, but there are some things that must always remain non-negotiable both in our individual lives, and also for our lives as the people of God.

These things which must remain unchanged, are non-negotiable, not because they have always been done this way. Nor yet are they non-negotiable, because they are our traditions. They are non-negotiable because the Word of God sets them down as essential truths, essential life style choices, essential characteristics to embrace. Where the Word of God sets anything down as essential, as the thing that God will bless, then no matter how long they have been believed, practised and done that way, we must not seek to budge and move those boundaries or we will miss out on the very blessing of living in the promises, presence and power of the living God.

The writer of Proverbs 22:28 wrote:

> *Do not move the ancient landmark that your fathers have set.*

In writing that proverb he used a word which although translated as 'landmark' may be better translated by the word 'boundary.' It speaks of a boundary enclosing territory, of a wall around an area. There will always be non negotiables and boundaries in our Christian faith, which will not suit the Perizzite spirit.

The being of our God is non-negotiable. The holiness and purity of our God is non-negotiable. The humanity and deity of Jesus the Christ is non-negotiable. The blood which Jesus shed, to pay the debt we owe to God and which alone cleanses us from sin is non-negotiable.

On the other hand there are things that do change. The way we look has changed. It would be completely absurd for us to walk around looking the same as the people of God looked in Joshua's day. The language we use, the clothes we wear, all these external trappings will change. Yet still, even though they change they must also always be kept within some non-negotiable boundaries. Things like foul language, taking the name of God lightly, dressing in ways that are provocative, will never be appropriate as we seek to emulate the way Jesus would live and speak were He walking the earth in our day.

The way we worship, the things we do, the methods and styles we adopt may change, but even here there are elements which must remain non-negotiable. It does not appear to matter whether we use no musical instruments, an organ, a piano, a violin, a guitar, a drum or even a whole orchestra. The instruments do not appear to make a lot of difference, either in the scriptures or through the history of the people of God. God seems to come and bless in any and all of those kinds of settings. None of those things seem to be significant. But the reality of worshipping God in spirit and in truth is still essential. Part of that requires us to lift our voices in song.

It probably does not matter whether we stand up to sing, or sit down to sing. I am not certain that God is particularly interested in whether we stand up to pray or kneel down to pray. It seems to make little difference to the one who looks on the thoughts and intents of our hearts. But this I know, when we come before Him, as we must do, both individually and collectively, there ought to be some singing, there has to be some prayer. In all of it we must acknowledge we come before a holy God who alone is worthy of our worship. There are some things that are non-negotiable.

But the Perizzite will come and desire us to change all things. He knows no bounds, he just wants to change things. So they will seek to remove the boundaries, and the essentials, often with a 'spiritual' sounding reason, sometimes with a mere claim that things have moved on and need to change if God's people are to keep up to date, and still be relevant in the world we live in.

Then the next thing about the Perizzite wanting to live without bounds is this. He will come with a desire to kick over all the traces and boundaries in personal lives and holiness. He does not believe in any form of restraint. There is nothing he will not do. The motto of the Perizzite spirit becomes something like this; "It is alright as long as it feels good", or "It is fine as long as it is enjoyable". They claim "It is acceptable as long as it does not hurt anybody", and "It is reasonable as long as somebody else has been happy for it to happen." It is an attempt to turn us off of God and bring us to live without restraint.

The truth the Perizzite will seek to attack here, is the use of the word sin, especially that word transgression, which speaks about crossing the line. God says there is a line, a boundary, which He has set in place. The Perizzite says the boundaries are shifting in this modern world. He will seek to persuade us that God did not really intend us to be so narrow and outdated in our views, thoughts and actions.

The Perizzite comes to seek to persuade us that whatever we do really does not matter because even if it is wrong, the grace of God is boundless, it is without limit. So even if it is against the teaching of the Scripture, it really does not matter, God will still be able to reach you.

The Apostle Paul challenged this kind of Perizzite spirit when he wrote to the church in Rome;

> *What shall we say then? Are we to continue in sin that grace may abound? By no means! How can we who died to sin still live in it?* Romans 6:1-2

But the Perizzite will try to persuade us that the love of God would not want to limit our pleasure, or deny our natural instincts, or our persona, so surely God would allow us to do whatever we choose as long as we enjoy it.

The Perizzite mindset will use phrases which they say are logical arguments against the old fashioned notions of transgression, iniquity, sin, wrong doing, evil habits and actions. They use arguments like these, "as long as it is fun"; "as long as it is enjoyable." "it is just the way I am." "I was born this way." "It hurts nobody." The only truth in any of it, is the truth that we were born that way. The psalmist declares we were born in sin and shaped in iniquity (Psalm 51:5). Other than that truth, which they would rather ignore, all their arguments are lies. The truth is that when we begin to live without restraint we will walk away from the ways of God, away from the person of the living God and away from the life that God says is the happiest and most blessed way to experience all He wants to give us.

The Perizzite mindset creeps up on us in this way. Something happens, and then later, as we are reading and meditating on the Bible, we realise that what we thought, what we did, or what we wanted was not in line with the will, ways and purposes of God. Now the Perizzite mindset will not want to come to terms with that. So rather than going to God in contrition and repentance, it seeks to turn us off of God. Instead of going and speaking with God about what we have read, we try to excuse or justify ourselves, first to ourselves, and then often to others around us.

Having gone that far we begin to take opportunities to express our point of view, to say why we can do, or think, or want, what the Bible seems to be against, and once we have done that, we feel better about it. But actually even as we do those things we have moved away from God, and the Perizzite spirit that came against us, is beginning to gain an upper hand in our lives.

Then the Perizzite spirit will suggest that what we want, what we desire and what we are involved in, will not hurt us or do us any harm. God comes and seeks to convict us, but as the Perizzite way of thinking takes root in our lives, we silence the promptings of the Holy Spirit within us. Before long we finish up living outside of the boundaries which God set for our eternal good, without the restraints of the Spirit of God on our consciences, and choosing to live just to please ourselves.

Soon after that, we reach the stage where, when we think something, we say it, when we feel like something, we do it, when we see something we want, we go out to get it.

We loose sight of the truth of God, the boundaries He set and the consequences of living without restraint. The devil is a liar. He will come and tell us that it will not hurt us, even as he did when he lied to Eve back in the garden of Eden. All he really wants to do is pick us up, chew us over, and then spit us out, leaving us with a life which is little more than a mere existence, far from God, miserable and in despair, feeling there is no way to ever enjoy life and God again.

The Lord Jesus Christ told a story. It is a remarkable story for many reasons. It is the story of a young man who just wanted to enjoy his life, without the restraints and boundaries he felt were upon him. So he went to his father and said, "You know, when you die, I'm going to have a lot of money. I want it now, I don't want to have to wait for it, I want to enjoy the present and live life to the full. Thank you very much." His father gave him the inheritance he asked for, and the young man went off to enjoy life.

He thought that enjoying life would satisfy him. What he did not remember was that the only way you can satisfy your soul and enjoy life is to live within the boundaries God has sets in His Word. He had not realised those boundaries were actually there to bless, not to spoil life.

So the young man went off to seek pleasure and enjoyment. He appeared to be having a good time, he appeared to have a lot of friends, he appeared to be enjoying life; until one day things changed. What he had depended on disappeared and he found himself poor, wretched, in despair, eating with the pigs in their trough.

I do not know if you have ever been to see pigs. Despite what people say they are not really dirty animals, it is just they choose not to live in the cleanest of conditions. But pigs will eat anything. It is one of the things that mark them out. They just eat whatever is there. They eat by putting their snouts into the trough or into the mud. Pigs go along and eat whatever is on the ground. They do not even look at what they are eating, they just eat whatever they find.

Jesus does not say how long the young man spent living in poverty and eating with the pigs. We cannot tell how long he lived in the field, in the mud, in the mire, wallowing in the grime along with the pigs. However long it was, Jesus said eventually he came to his senses and said "this life is not what I was expecting. This is not the enjoyment I was looking for."

It really does not matter what particular boundary we want to cross, which limit we want to ignore and kick over. It is possible that your thing is the same as mine, it is possible yours is completely different to mine. It really makes very little difference. What is guaranteed is that the Perizzite spirit will come and try to convince us that whatever it is, will not hurt, and will not harm. It will be fun, enjoyable, and it should at least be tried. Surely, we should be able to try everything once.

But, the devil has always been a liar and is the father of lies. Whenever we cross the boundary that God has set, it will harm us. It will hurt us. It will damage us. It will take us and turn us off of the living God. We will find ourselves eventually wallowing in dirt, wondering how ever we finished up so far from God.

The Apostle Paul addresses the issues in Romans 3 he says "There is none righteous, no, not one." Go back a couple of chapters to the first chapter of Romans and see what the Apostle Paul says;

> *For although they knew God, they did not honor him as God or give thanks to him, but they became futile in their thinking, and their foolish hearts were darkened. Claiming to be wise, they became fools, and exchanged the glory of the immortal God for images resembling mortal man and birds and animals and creeping things. Romans 3:21-22*

Then he continues;

> *And since they did not see fit to acknowledge God, God gave them up to a debased mind to do what ought not to be done. They were filled with all manner of unrighteousness, evil, covetousness, malice. They are full of envy, murder, strife, deceit, maliciousness. They are gossips, slanderers, haters of God, insolent, haughty, boastful, inventors of evil, disobedient to parents, foolish, faithless, heartless, ruthless. Though they know God's righteous decree that those who practice such things deserve to die, they not only do them but give approval to those who practice them.*
> *Romans 3:28-32*

Here is where the Perizzite spirit will take us. It will make us want to read these lists of things which cross the boundaries God set, and allow us to concentrate on certain ones, normally the lines we have no desire to cross.

He will do that and then persuade us that we have not crossed any of those lines. The truth is that somewhere in the list we can discover the weakness, the propensity found in our hearts which will lead us from walking in the ways of God.

The Perizzite spirit will always want to pick on the parts of the list that are not our weakness and make us rejoice that at least we are not like that. The reality is that when we do this, all we are really doing is seeking to justify ourselves in a self-righteous and hypocritical manner. There is none righteous, no not one. God comes to us and pleads with us not to live without boundaries.

We are just going to notice six scriptures which set out ways to fight the Perizzite spirit as it comes to seek to invade our thinking.

First, let us know that the fear of the Lord, the reverence for his being and his name, is the beginning of wisdom. He is an awesome God. He is a holy God. He is a pure God. You and I are answerable to this God. Reverence his name. Begin to acknowledge his power and his being.

> *The fear of the Lord is the beginning of wisdom; all those who practice it have a good understanding. Psalm 111:10.*

Second, we must realize that we do not belong to ourself. We are not free to do just whatever we choose to do. We are people who belong to God;

> *You are not your own, for you were bought with a price. So glorify God in your body.*
> *1 Corinthians 9:19-20*

Third, we need to acknowledge that all we really need for our good and for real lasting enjoyment comes from the hand of the Lord God and by His grace.

> *Trust in the living God, who giveth us richly all things to enjoy; 1 Timothy 6:17*

Then realise and acknowledge we do not need the pleasures of sin, which only last for a season anyway. Instead let us always have an eye on the recompense of the reward. Look at the life of Moses. He knew that God was able to bless him more than any blessing he could find elsewhere.

> *choosing rather to be mistreated with the people of God than to enjoy the fleeting pleasures of sin. He considered the reproach of Christ greater wealth than the treasures of Egypt, for he was looking to the reward. Hebrews 11:25-26*

Recognize the value and importance of the revelation of God. That revelation which has been given to us, both in Jesus, the living Word and in the scripture, His written word.

> *Thy word Oh lord is a light to my feet and a lamp to my path. Psalm 109:105*

God's word is there for us in order that we may know, with absolute certainty how we ought to live day by day. We need to keep our Bible open, to read our Bible day by day, and never allow it to be kept closed from week to week. Even as we need food for our bodies, we need God's word to nourish us day by day

Fifth, acknowledge that God's Word is absolute truth.

Nothing within it was ever written to make our pleasure less. It was written to make our pleasures pure, unbridled, holy and complete.

> *Blessed is the man who walks not in the counsel of the wicked, nor stands in the way of sinners, nor sits in the seat of scoffers; but his delight is in the law of the Lord, and on his law he meditates day and night. He is like a tree planted by streams of water that yields its fruit in its season, and its leaf does not wither. In all that he does, he prospers. Psalm 1:1-3*

Finally, always immerse ourself in the Lord our God at every opportunity we have.

> *You shall love the LORD your God with all your heart and with all your soul and with all your might. Deuteronomy 6:5*

I have a problem with the day and culture in which I live. Worship services are around an hour and a quarter maybe an hour and a half. We are told that people cannot concentrate for longer than that. Yet many will go to the cinema and watch a film for two hours without complaining. Most will follow a television series and watch each programme for two hours and at the end are excited and expectant for the next episode. Nothing will make them forget to catch the next episode and in case they may miss it, they record it. Then find time in the week to catch up with that recording. But a service, a prayer meeting, our own private daily times with God!

As we immerse ourselves in God, He will keep us from living without boundaries. God will put the restraints in place and cause us to walk in His path knowing that He is not against us. He is for us. He is on our side.

The Perizzite spirit is a giant out to get us. He wants to suggest that God puts too many restraints in our way and we can just ignore them. He wants to suggest that God is a killjoy, a mean and uncaring God. He has been trying the same trick ever since the garden of Eden. Never debate with him, never listen to his lies. Know and understand, the only way to truly enjoy life is to recognize that the Lord our God is able to do all we need and more on top of that, to bring us real and lasting pleasure.

I remember one day going to collect my mother for church. She was in a nursing home and suffering from the onset of dementia. I got there late, but when I arrived to pick her up she had no coat on. She was dressed in just a skirt and a top. So I told her it was cold out and she needed her coat. We went upstairs to her room to find a coat. On the way back down we passed one of the nursing staff. They asked her if she was going off to church and she said yes. The nurse said "well enjoy yourself." As my mother started to walk down the stairs, she turned to me and said, "What a terrible thing to say. Fancy going to church to enjoy yourself." Now do not misunderstand me, she loved the Lord her God, she used to spend the whole of her week waiting for the next Sunday, but her mind had started to fail. But as I thought about her words that morning, I realised how easy it is to get to that point where we come to worship out of duty, rather than from the joy of being in God's presence among His people.

All too quickly we loose sight of the God who has loved

us with an everlasting love. A God who loved us so much that He gave to us and for us. He gave His Son into this world to free us from our sin to free us from the burden of our sin, to break the power of sin upon us, to remove the guilt and weight of sin from us. He has done that, and now He reaches out in loving kindness to find ways to help us day by day.

Immerse yourself in God. Love the Lord your God. Be where his heart is. Love to be where His heart is. Delight in being where His eyes are. Where His children meet together.

Know that as we meet to worship, His heart is among us, and His eyes watch over us. Keep within the boundaries God sets. Not because someone else says it, not from fear of being found out and exposed, but because we love the Lord who set those boundaries for our good, and because the Word of God says 'walk this way, and you will walk in life'. 'Walk a different way and you will walk astray, into sorrow, despair and ultimately into death'. Let us be people who always choose life.

Girgashites

God has reached into our lives and into our world in order to help us, bless us, and provide for us in ways we need. To take away our sin, to watch over us day by day, and to bring us into His promises, so that we might live the abundant life He intended for us.

There is an enemy of souls who seeks to bring things to our attention with the aim of keeping us from walking into that abundant life. He brings attitudes, mindsets, paradigms, and desires. All of them seeking to keep us from that life which God had prepared and purposed for us.

As we turn to the fifth of those nations of giants who aim to keep God's people from inheriting the promises we come to the schemes of the Girgashites.

Girgashites are not only found in the Old Testament. This nation is also found in the New Testament, but there the writers use the Aramaic equivalent of the Hebrew word. That Aramaic name is the word Gadarene or sometimes spelled Gerasene. It is the same nation. Since there is reference to them in the Gospels, we can look there to help us understand the devices and schemes they use, and the mindset they espouse. The word Girgashite means 'clay dwellers'.

Always remember these names are not there to criticize certain people groups. Certainly we are not intended to judge those who live in mud or clay buildings.

The name Girgashite is there to help us understand the danger of the mindset which tries to enter and eventually control us, whether we live in clay buildings or large stone mansions. This name means clay dwellers, or it can be translated just as accurately as 'earth dwellers.'

The Girgashite spirit speaks of a mindset, a way of thinking, a paradigm for life, where the only thing to be considered or concerned with in life, is the earth, or the clay in which we dwell.

Particularly in this twenty first century it is necessary to point out that while the Girgashite spirit speaks about being concerned for the earth or the clay in which we dwell, it is not intended to be seen as any kind of statement or criticism about those who have a concern for environmental or green issues. To think like that would be completely to miss the point of God's desire to drive out this nation before us.

We can underline the fact that this is not intended to suggest we should not be concerned about environmental issues since the God who placed us on the earth, also gave instruction for us to look after that earth. All of us live on the earth. God is not saying we should not live here. We all live on the earth, and He gave us the responsibility to look after, to care for, and to manage the earth He placed us in. We are stewards of all He made.

The Girgashite spirit is, however, a spirit which is described as being an earth dwelling, or clay dwelling spirit.

As we come to think about this name, perhaps the first thing to remind ourselves of comes from the very creation of mankind. God took of the earth, of the mud, and made man and then breathed into man the breath of life.

This Girgashite spirit thinks only about the mud we were made from and the clay we live in and around, It chooses to ignore the breath of God, the spirit of the Lord which was breathed into that clay to give life to the mud.

The Girgashite mindset encourages us to only ever think about this earthbound life. It is a mindset which only allows for thought and consideration to be given to elements based upon this temporal earth and our physical being. Only this temporal and material thinking is allowed to govern and move the heart and mind of a person.

That mindset, that attitude, and that paradigm is described by this word Girgashite. It is a mindset that only thinks about what can be seen, as though there is no reality to be found in anything other than what can be seen and touched. It sees nothing beyond this material earth and the arena of time.

All the Girgashite thinks about, the only things they talk about, and the only things that turns them on, are the things going on in this material world. They give no thought to anything else. They are people who are taken up with the visible, provable material Earth. They are earth bound and time bound, Girgashites.

They consider any people claiming to be the people of

God to be deluded, foolish, and of no use in this world. They consider them ignorant of the realities of life. The Girgashite talks of those who claim to be in relationship with God as people who are of no earthly use, because they are deluded, taken up with a fiction of some other world. They not only talk like that, they have a passionate desire to ensure that everyone they meet should consider nothing real, apart from this material, time governed world.

Every plan they make is based on the here and now, all the interests they have are based on this earth, and the things of this earth. They live, and even begin to think of themselves as nothing more than an animal species which has evolved over time on this planet.

The Apostle Paul wrote about this mindset in his letter to the church in Philippi.

> *Their end is destruction, their god is their belly, and their glory is in their shame. Their minds are set on earthly things. Philippians 3:19*

When he writes 'their god is their belly,' it does not mean that God did not intend us to enjoy our food. Nor does it mean we do not like to have something sensible to drink. But christian people recognise there is a limit to what food and drink can do for us. We also know that if we go too far, food and drink, far from helping us can actually damage us. We know there is a value in moderation, but the Girgashite does not think about moderation in any activity. They are consumed with this world. Their whole concern is for the here and now, this present existence.

I remember seeing a couple of people out running one day. Now, I am not against exercise, but these men looked as though they really needed to be wheeled round rather than trying to run. I stopped one of them. He was red, I mean he was almost purple, from his head to his toes. It looked as if though any moment he might suffer some fatal attack. I stopped him to chat, and asked why he felt the need to run at that rate. He said he was running like that in order to prolong life as long as he could.

Let us be clear, we should not be opposed to exercise, it is a necessary part of the life we have. The Bible says 'bodily exercise profits a little'. It is also true that exercise needs to increase the heart rate and the blood flow to be of real benefit to our bodies. But it sometimes seems as though there are people who are completely caught up in trying to prolong this life, as though the only reality is this life, this world, this earth, this natural existence. They live a dangerous existence spending all their time and expending all their energy caring for their bodies but forgetting their immortal souls.

The Girgashite will say he would be willing to believe in God, if His existence could be proved. They think this earth came into being by chance. They think everything in this world is the result of some chance happening, either some evolutionary result, or some other coincidental event.

Now personally, I think believing that everything is here just by chance, or by evolution over aeons of time, needs a bigger step of faith than believing in the activity of a living God who created all things. It is no more possible to prove any of their those ideas, than it is to prove the existence of God. Both require a leap into the unknown and an acceptance of reasoned evidence, mysteries and uncertain theories. Personally I think the recognition of a God who made the world and all that is in it, seems not only to be true, based on His word, but is also the best explanation for all the variety and wonder of the creation around us.

But the Girgashite declares that because the existence of God cannot be 'scientifically' proven, they cannot believe in Him. They claim that because God cannot be seen, He cannot exist. They forget that the invisible God, became visible and entered our world in the person of Jesus the Christ, in order that God should be seen and known, and everyone might realise that God is good and does good.

That is not enough for the Girgashite. Faced with the person of Jesus Christ, with the evidence before them, that Jesus was God and did good, they just desire to be left alone.

There is a story about Girgashites in the New Testament. There were two poor men, bound in chains, and bound by a violent spirit, running around naked in the area where they dwelt, they lived among the graves, in the place of the dead.

Jesus came across the Sea of Galilee and came ashore at the place where these poor men were chained. Finding the men in this sorry condition, He healed them, freed them from bondage, physical, mental and spiritual bondage. The two men were suddenly in their right mind, freed from their animalistic nature and made human, wholly human, trusting in God.

The gospel account tells us that when the rest of the Gadarenes, (the Girgashites) saw what had happened, they asked Jesus to leave quickly. They asked no question about how this had happened, they made no enquiry about why anyone had cared enough to solve the poor men's tragic condition. They just made a request for Jesus, the Son of God, to go away so they could all just be left alone. They begged Jesus to go!

The Girgashite is the kind of person who is scared to come into a church in case even walking through the doors might do them some hurt. How illogical, if you do not believe in the supernatural. How strange if you really think there is no God. After all the church building is just another building. There is this inconsistency in the way they live as just material beings in a material world, and yet what they are, troubles them.

They try to ignore the fact that there is more to life than this body. They want to live with no thought for God. No thought for the reality that mankind is more than just flesh and blood. No thought for their immortal souls, blinded into thinking we are no more than animals who live on this earth, die and go back to the dust.

But the truth is, we are not just animals. We are more than that. We are not created equal with any animal, however lovely, cute or strong they may be. We are not created equal with any other creatures on the planet. God made us, yes out of the dirt, but when He had done that, he took the mud man He had created and breathed His spirit into man. In doing that He made us in His own image and breathed immortality into mankind.

> *He has made everything beautiful in its time. Also, he has put eternity into man's heart, Ecclesiastes 3:11*

He put eternity into our hearts. He made us, that we might know Him as the only living God and that we might live in fellowship with Him day by day, both in this world and also in the world which is still to come.

If we allow the Girgashite spirit to enter into our way of living and thinking, so that we begin to only think in terms of what can be seen and handled and then fail to think about the eternity of the living God and the eternal destination of our immortal souls, that Girgashite mindset spirit will do what all the giant nations seek to do. It will not just turn us off from God. It will not even just take us away from living in the fullness of the promises of God. It will destroy our souls, our very life.

The story of those two poor men in Matthew 8, who had lived among the Girgashites for so long, tells us that they were inhabited by legions of giants. When Jesus came to heal them, the legions of giants asked Jesus for permission to go and live in the pigs if they had to leave these poor men alone. Jesus allowed this and as soon as the legions had entered the pigs, they immediately took all the pigs headlong over a cliff to their deaths.

Those Girgashite spirits desired to be allowed to enter the pigs when Jesus called them out of the two men. There is a difference between that attitude, to be among pigs, and the attitude of the people of God, who are so often described as the sheep, as the flock of God.

There is a basic difference between pigs and sheep which I just mention here. Pigs will happily wallow in mud, in the dirt, in the mire, while sheep will cry out until they are brought out of the mire. With that thought, let us think about some truths we need to remember in order to avoid allowing the entrance of a Girgashite mindset into our way of living.

Always remember we have an immortal soul. We are not just a body, we also have an immortal soul and God has put eternity into our hearts. One of the proofs of that scripture which demonstrates the eternity in our hearts and our immortal souls can be seen in the way that we never seem to feel older. We get an awareness that our outward bodies are ageing. But on our good days, we still feel the same age as we have for years. It is only looking in a mirror that makes us realize time is passing. The almost universal recognition among mankind, in the face of death, that death is not the end is a further reminder of the immortal soul and the truth of eternity God placed within us all.

Then we need to ensure we are never in a position where we are tempted to run away from the person of Jesus, or from the presence of the living God. It is one of the lovely things that differentiated a children from adults when Jesus walked upon the face of the earth. The children were always found running to Jesus.

We read that one day, as the children were running to Jesus, the disciples got upset and said they should not do that. The answer of Jesus is worth pondering. He said that unless we are like a child, we will never get to the kingdom of heaven. Understand, He was telling the disciples we should always be found running and coming to God and never be found trying to run away from Him.

The Lord Jesus Christ came into the world and lived in the world and died upon a cross to save us from our sins. He did all that was necessary to bring us into relationship with a living God. Never run from Him. Never be like the Girgashites and say, 'Please go away from us. We don't want this Jesus here.' Run towards Him. He is the one who has cared for you and provided for you.

Never be ashamed of Jesus. Luke 9:25-26:

> *For what does it profit a man if he gains the whole world and loses or forfeits himself? For whoever is ashamed of me and of my words, of him will the Son of Man be ashamed when he comes in his glory and the glory of the Father and of the holy angels.*

Jesus explains for those who are ashamed of Him, there will come a day when they stand before the living God and in that day Jesus says He will be ashamed to acknowledge them. Those who have run from Him, He will turn away from on that day.

Even if you gain the whole world, with a life centred on time and this world, you cannot take your sin away! You cannot take your guilt away! You cannot remove your condemnation! Never run from Him, Jesus came into the world for people like us.

> *The saying is trustworthy and deserving of full acceptance, that Christ Jesus came into the world to save sinners, of whom I am the foremost. 1 Timothy 1:15*

Let our minds be always thinking about Jesus the Christ and what He has done for us. He was the Son of God who loved us and gave Himself for us. We need to allow our minds to be filled with Jesus the Christ and His love for us and all it means for Him to say He came and gave Himself for us.

We need to keep in our minds the truth of eternity and all that eternity will mean for us. We have an immortal spirit so should keep the recognition of the immortal in our minds and thoughts. When the Apostle Peter came to write a letter to Christian people, he wrote

> *"I want you to know that all of my days, I'm going to keep reminding you of this, that God sent His Son into the world to save you. And to bring you into an eternity with himself. I'm going to make sure that all of the time, I keep saying it to you." Therefore I intend always to remind you of these qualities, though you know them and are established in the truth that you have. I think it right, as long as I am in this body, to stir you up by way of reminder, since I know that the putting off of my body will be soon, as our Lord Jesus Christ made clear to me. And I will make every effort so that after my departure you may be able at any time to recall these things. 2 Peter 1:12-15;*

The reason Peter said he would always bring this truth before people is just that we so easily forget. All too quickly we get taken up with the world and the things in the world. We have this tendency to loose sight of the realities of life and eternity and begin to live as though this world is all there is, and the Girgashite mindset encroaches on our very beings.

Charles Spurgeon was reputed to have said that he had 1000 texts, but all of them talked about Jesus Christ. Jesus said that all the scriptures talk about Him. They talk about faith in Him and about eternity, they talk about how to live in this world in a way that blesses others and end our days walking into an eternity with the living God. The truths in those scriptures will only impact us as we take the time to read, study and meditate upon them.

Always keep your mind fixed on the unseen world and the eternal God rather than the seen and the temporal parts of life.

> *we look not to the things that are seen but to the things that are unseen. For the things that are seen are transient, but the things that are unseen are eternal. 2 Corinthians 4:18.*

The Apostle Paul writing there, speaks about some of the problems and difficulties he has faced, and then says in effect, "You know what? All the things that happen in this world, they are all changing, they are all temporary, they are all passing. But the things of God are eternal, they will never change." A number of times, over the fourth and fifth chapter of this second letter to the church in Corinth, he repeats a statement saying "we do not loose heart", "we are confident". This security of his heart and confidence he attributes to the eternal realm and the spiritual realities he keeps before him.

When we come into fellowship with the living God, we are to live with an eye to investing in our eternity. When we come to know Jesus Christ for ourselves, we are changing our destiny for eternity. Let us fill our minds with eternity and keep our mind fixed on the things that will never change. Everything else in this world is changing. Nothing in this world is certain or fixed. But the spiritual realm is certain and heaven is unmoveable and unshakable.

The Girgashite comes to tell us that it is not wise to trust in things we cannot see. They want to convince us to only believe in what is scientifically proveable.

All too often they are speaking of something which the Bible says is falsely called science.[1] To talk about life and the universe in which we dwell, you have to know what started things and what works in things. You have to understand the origin of things and the sustaining of things. The only answer for all of that is found in the reality of the living God.

We need wisdom to understand these things. We must ensure we have real wisdom, and keep our minds fixed on that wisdom, which comes from the living God.

> *Who is wise and understanding among you? By his good conduct let him show his works in the meekness of wisdom. But if you have bitter jealousy and selfish ambition in your hearts, do not*

[1] See illustrations of science proved wrong, page 127-128.

> *boast and be false to the truth. This is not the wisdom that comes down from above, but is earthly, unspiritual, demonic. For where jealousy and selfish ambition exist, there will be disorder and every vile practice. But the wisdom from above is first pure, then peaceable, gentle, open to reason, full of mercy and good fruits, impartial and sincere. And a harvest of righteousness is sown in peace by those who make peace. James 3:13-18*

The world paradigm, the earth thinking, the sensual animalistic attitude, will seek to make us deny our immortal spirit and eternal destiny with God. It will try to make us so taken up with this world, it's times, and it's fashions that we walk away from the living God. Let us avoid it, put a void between the Girgashite and us, and let our wisdom be pure, peaceable, gentle, always easy to be entreated, always willing to be moved into the way of God, never running from Him but always running to Him and the Girgashite spirit will run from us.

Amorites

We turn our attention next to this sixth nation of giants, the Amorites. In the same way each of the other nations of giants still exist, the Amorites are also still around us. They can be found organising the way the world runs, and organising the way the world thinks.

As we look at the Amorite nation and follow the word 'amorite' through the Old Testament, we find this reference to them in the prophecy of Amos. Amos records this message from God concerning this nation:

> *"Yet it was I who destroyed the Amorite before them, whose height was like the height of the cedars and who was as strong as the oaks; I destroyed his fruit above and his roots beneath. Also it was I who brought you up out of the land of Egypt and led you forty years in the wilderness, to possess the land of the Amorite." Amos 2:9-10*

God was still reminding His people, years after Moses and Joshua, that these Amorites are giants, taller than the cedar trees and stronger than an oak tree. We dare not attack them alone, for we will never manage to overcome and destroy them without the help of the living God. But He has promised to drive them out before us and He also still expects us to push them away.

Through the prophet Amos God says, He is still able to help us destroy the Amorites. There God sets out the way He will do this. He says He will treat them like a tree. He will chop off the bit at the top that grows fruit and seeds.

At the same time He will chop through the roots of the tree. When you cut both the top and the root from a tree, the part in-between is ready to die. In this way, God declares, He will offer us victory over this giant.

There are a number of things to learn from the meaning of this word Amorite, in order to spot their mindset when it comes against us seeking to overpower us. Only when we see the danger coming will we ask God to help us deal with it, before it manages to take root in our minds and hearts.

The word Amorite comes from the word 'to say', but it has something else added to it. The primary root meaning is 'to say in prominence' or 'to speak in prominence'.

Because it had the concept of prominence, and speaking from a position of prominence, over time it came to refer to "mountain dwellers". As we have noted before, this is not a literal prohibition on a particular dwelling location. We may choose to live in a mountain area. That is not the issue. The word Amorite only came to refer to mountain dwellers because of this idea of taking a position of prominence or superior power, from where they would choose to speak.

It is that thought of prominence, of holding a position above others and speaking from that position of power which is central to the Amorite spirit.

The person with an Amorite mindset always think themselves better than others. It thinks they are more important than anybody else. They believe they should take a place of prominence, and importance. The person with an Amorite spirit comes and think themselves better than others, because of their belief that their actions or abilities are more significant than other peoples. They parade their sense of importance and status.

The Amorite spirit encourages a mind that is puffed up. Because of that you tend to find, when talking to someone with an Amorite mindset, they always seem to be speaking down to everyone. They have a patronising tone as they deal with those of us who are mere ordinary humans. If they take on a religious nature they will be heard thanking God that they are not like the rest of the people. They will thank God that they are by nature so much better than others.

It is easy to spot those with an Amorite spirit outside of church circles. Inside church circles it can become more complex to spot. In our own hearts and minds there are dangers which can flow from this superior belief which we will do well to spot early and repent of speedily. The Amorite spirit sometimes shows itself like this. It suggests that others would be as far along the path with God as they are, if only they had known and had the experiences they have or, moved in the same circles they have, or even, if only they had experienced the feelings and emotions they have been blessed to see in their lives. It is always based on the false notion that they are as they are because of something innately in them.

My father used to tell the story of a person who one day early on in life had an experience of God. The experience so impressed him that he wrote it down. Nothing wrong with writing a journal of your walk in life. So far no issue arises. But then whenever anyone went to see him, he got out his written account of the experience and read it to his visitors. Before long, people stopped going to see him because they got tired of hearing about something that had happened to him so many years ago.

Just as an aside we need to always ensure our testimony is a fresh testimony and that it gives glory to God, not to us. It is supposed to be about what God has done, not just years ago but what He has done this week or today. God desires to touch our lives every day.

People became tired of going to see the man my father spoke of, because they did not want to hear again, the story of what God did for him years ago, which he believed had set him apart as special, unique.

After many years passed, he was taken ill and his pastor went to visit him. As soon as the pastor walked through the door, the man asked to be allowed to read about the experience he had years before and said, "you know, I'm so much better than most of your people, because I had an experience in my 20's." He went to the cupboard to get the paper that he had written all those years before, but when he looked it was shredded to pieces, because the mice had eaten their way through the paper. He cried out, "oh, what can I do, the mice have eaten my experience!"

That is kind of a silly story. But there is a grain of truth within it. There really are people who think of themselves as better because they have gone through certain things. There are others who consider themselves more significant because they have achieved certain things. Others who feel they deserve great recognition because of something in their lives which they look back on, or even just because of their background. Worse than any of that they look down on the rest of humanity. They all come to a place where they feel able to look down on people, who are just struggling on every day. It is an Amorite Spirit. The tragedy is this. The pride it encourages becomes the very thing that God hates and it is the attitude that finds itself being resisted by God.

This Amorite mindset is common in many of the gospel narratives. See what the Lord Jesus had to say about it. Because every time he came across Pharisees, who thought of themselves as better than the rest, the Lord Jesus spoke to them in devastating ways.

> *"Woe to you, scribes and Pharisees, hypocrites! For you are like whitewashed tombs, which outwardly appear beautiful, but within are full of dead people's bones and all uncleanness. So you also outwardly appear righteous to others, but within you are full of hypocrisy and lawlessness." Matthew 23:27-28*

He called them a load of whited sepulchers, rotten from the inside out. Then you find him telling them they stink! Jesus had that habit of talking absolutely straight to people and addressing them just where they were. It was not always pleasant for them to hear what He had to say.

We need to always remember of ourselves we are nothing. Every experience, every skill, every talent, every understanding we have comes not because we are so good, so great or so cute. It only ever comes through the grace of the living God. Remember, grace is when you receive what you do not deserve, when you experience what you do not earn and when you discover what you could not know apart from the unmerited favour and goodness of God.

We can also find this tendency to make way for an Amorite spirit when we come to think about sin. This is especially true when we come to think about certain particular sins within the world. Most people, when they talk about sin, talk about the ones which are not their weakness. They tend to talk more often, and more easily, about the wickedness of sin when they can name sins they have never struggled with.

The truth is, that outside of God's grace all of us are lost, and even within the grace of God, all of us have enough problems dealing with the sin which is our particular weakness, without picking on the sins of others. All of us, if we are Christian people, are at best sinners saved by grace.

The real danger with this Amorite spirit is seen in the pride it spawns. The greatest spiritual peril can overtake us whenever we start to think that we are better than others. Before long, we struggle to think there is anything wrong within us at all. We begin to concentrate on the way we have overcome the sins that others struggle with, the ones we happily mention, and forget that we are struggling with attitudes, feelings, habits, emotions which are just as far from the perfection of a holy and just God.

Before long, we think we are overcomers of all that is wrong, but we are deluded and will soon find ourselves far away from God.

Pride is one of the attitudes of heart which we struggle with all the days of our lives. Just when we think we have overcome it, something happens and suddenly it rears it's head once more.

Encouraging one another is a good thing, but there is a danger in it for us. Somebody comes and praises us, or thanks us for something we have done. Suddenly we feel our chest puff out, and pride sneaks back in and we think to ourself, as we agree with them, that we deserve the praise, we did so well. We need to understand and remember, if ever we do anything well, it is because of the grace of God enabling us, and the ability of the Spirit of Jesus working within us. He, alone, deserves the praise.

We have already mentioned the truth that God resists the proud. It says it twice in the New Testament. It is in the Epistle of James, and it is also recorded in the Epistle of Peter. That should give us a clue not only about how dangerous an attitude pride is, but also how common it was among the early believers.

It was the first sin which entered the universe when Satan was puffed up with pride. He longs to see that same sin reproduced in men and women. It is terrible when you see it in anybody who is so proud and arrogant that they think they are better than the rest. It is worse when you see it among brothers and sisters in Christ who think of themselves as better than others. They become religious fools, self righteous, arrogant people, a blight upon the gospel, and upon the world.

There is further danger found in the root of this word Amorite. The whole idea of desiring acceptance and recognition is found at the root of this word. This giant comes to foster an unhealthy longing for fame. Andy Warhol is quoted as saying, "In the future, everyone will be world-famous for 15 minutes".

The world feeds that fallen desire for fame, and for all that comes with it. As I write this, there is a firm on the internet who promise to 'sell people a crowd, in order that they can make a person famous for a day'. The desire for fame has created a host of television shows, whose sole idea is to take ordinary people, put them on the world stage and make them famous. The whole world is moved by this desire to try and become famous. They offer to make stars overnight, without any of the background, any of the ability, any of the counseling or guidance needed to help them cope with being pushed into the spotlight, without becoming proud and arrogant. They make them popular for a day, and then the next day have no concern if they are then forgotten.

When Satan gets you to the pinnacle of pride and ability, at the end of the day, he will chew you up and spit you out. He only ever comes to steal, to kill, and to destroy. Those who reach the heights of prominence often finish in the depths of being unknown, forgotten. There is no lasting satisfaction or joy to be found in popularity or fame.

We need to be careful what we wish for. We can reach the heights because of some gifting that God has given to us. But if we lose sight of the fact that it is the living God who gifted us, and fail to give Him praise for all that He has done for us, the Amorite spirit will enter our mind, and we will become proud and arrogant, until one day we will be standing in prominence thinking we have achieved it all by ourself, and the enemy will have moved us away and turned us off of God.

Be careful, or you may find God will bring you down to the place of solitary confinement, out of the spotlight, humbled and alone.

There was a king one day. He came from a one time small and insignificant country. But he over ran and conquered the whole of what was the known world of his day. He rose to huge amounts of prominence and power because of the ability and skill he had been given. He was in charge of what had become one of the richest nations on the face of this earth at that time.

One day He was walking in his garden. As he walked in the garden, he looked out over the palace. He looked at all the wonders of the kingdom he now ruled and declared, "By my power, I have made this great kingdom for myself and by myself." In that moment, his wisdom left his brain. He began to live like an animal on the ground until his hair grew long and matted together. His nails grew so long, they came over the top like claws, and he was put out of the palace and away from the sight of all the people. He lived like that for a number of weeks, it ran into months, and then years, until one day, crawling around in the dirt on his hands and knees, eating the grass on the ground, he managed to look up. He lifted his gaze to the skies, to the heavens, towards the living God.

As he looked to God, he made a declaration. It is a declaration which should be acknowledged by all of us, but especially any who seek fame and prominence in any area of society. This is what he said;

> *I blessed the Most High, and praised and honored him who lives forever, for his dominion is an everlasting dominion, and his kingdom endures from generation to generation; all the inhabitants of the earth are accounted as nothing, and he does according to his will among the host of heaven and among the inhabitants of the earth; and none can stay his hand or say to him, "What have you done?"*

In looking to God and acknowledging Him alone, in that moment his wisdom returned, and he continued by saying:

> *At the same time my reason returned to me, and for the glory of my kingdom, my majesty and splendor returned to me. My counselors and my lords sought me, and I was established in my kingdom, and still more greatness was added to me. Now I, Nebuchadnezzar, praise and extol and honor the King of heaven, for all his works are right and his ways are just; and those who walk in pride he is able to humble. Daniel 4:34-37*

Be wary of the Amorite spirit and learn how to overcome it as soon as we feel it stirring in our heart, or whispering to our mind. Overcoming this giant is not easy, none of them are, but the Bible gives us weapons to use in the fight.

The first one is to remember that the God who resists the proud is the same God who gives grace to the humble.

> *Therefore humble yourselves under the mighty hand of God, James 4:10*

We need to always remind ourselves, we are nothing without Him, never think we are anything outside of God.

Remember we can do nothing without God. Understand, that is not the same as saying we cannot do anything, for there are all sorts of people doing all sorts of things without God. All they do will end up coming to nothing, unless God is in them, and is recognised and honoured as the source of what has been done.

> *I am the vine; you are the branches. Whoever abides in me and I in him, he it is that bears much fruit, for apart from me you can do nothing.*
> *John 15:5*

Acknowledge that the wisdom of this world, no matter how wonderful it appears, will never compete with the wisdom of the living God, 1 Corinthians 3:10.

Let me give a couple of quick examples of the wisdom of the world, which time has shown to be not only false, but absurdly stupid. In the 17th century there was a group of German scientists who had all been working together to create something called a railway train. In working on this, they looked at the scientific data they had and put out a paper to the whole of the rest of the scientific world. That paper gave their wisdom which said that if railway engines ever went faster than 25 miles an hour, everybody on board the train would develop a nosebleed.

A group of English scientists took that information as true, but went a little further. They said that if the train were to go into a tunnel and be in that tunnel for longer than three seconds, all the passengers inside would be likely to either suffocate or they would go mad. They also issued a paper around 1830, to say that when people saw steam engines for the first time, they were likely to go mad overnight, because they would not be able to comprehend how an iron machine could be made to move down another piece of iron.

There is also this truly wonderful example of scientific wisdom and understanding. When the YWCA first came into being, they decided they would help women learn to type. They announced they would run a typing course for women. Once that announcement had been made, there were a number of scientists in the United States who warned that they should not attempt to do this. Their reason to advise against this course of action, as leading scientists, was based on their conviction that "a women's frame is not capable of being a typist, if they start to press keys at any speed, their whole bodies will fall apart."

There was another group of scientists who claimed you would never be able to make boats out of metal, because metal cannot float, therefore they would always need to be made of wood.

So much of what the world's scientists and wise men have declared as absolute reality and truth, has over time diminished, been adjusted or even passed away completely. But every word the living God has declared has been shown to be true. His word alone is the one word which will prove to be true every time, in the end. The wisdom of this world does not compare with the wisdom of the God who made us and who knows us. He knows all about us and is fully aware of all that we need and require for life. We must acknowledge everything we read and encounter within that Word is there for our good. It is something to benefit us. Everything outside of God that we look to for wisdom, fame and fortune counts for nothing. Everything we think makes us something, outside of the grace and mercy of God, is worth nothing in the final reckoning.

It is that humility, and recognition which led the apostle Paul to write to the church in Philippi:

> *I myself have reason for confidence in the flesh also. If anyone else thinks he has reason for confidence in the flesh, I have more: circumcised on the eighth day, of the people of Israel, of the tribe of Benjamin, a Hebrew of Hebrews; as to the law, a Pharisee; as to zeal, a persecutor of the church; as to righteousness under the law, blameless. But whatever gain I had, I counted as loss for the sake of Christ. Indeed, I count everything as loss because of the surpassing worth of knowing Christ Jesus my Lord. For his sake I have suffered the loss of all things and count them as rubbish, in order that I may gain Christ and be found in him, not having a righteousness of my own that comes from*

> *the law, but that which comes through faith in Christ, the righteousness from God that depends on faith— that I may know him and the power of his resurrection, and may share his sufferings, becoming like him in his death, that by any means possible I may attain the resurrection from the dead. Philippians 3:1-11*

We must agree with the Apostle Paul, compared to the knowledge of knowing Jesus Christ, whatever the world has counted as something that is important to me, is nothing compared to knowing Him.

We should never think that we are anything special of ourselves, or that we have arrived in life. Every day is a day to discover more of God's truth, of the beauty of Jesus the Christ, of the wonder of the Scripture, and the miracle of our redemption and salvation. Every day God desires to show us new depths of truth. We are on a journey of discovery. We are in the place where at the moment we only ever know in part. The part we know God longs to increase within us, growing our heads and our hearts to become more like Jesus, until the day when we fully know, and are made altogether like Him. Until that day let him who thinks he stands take care lest he fall, thinking himself to be something becomes as nothing in the kingdom of God. (1 Corinthians 10:12, Galatians 6:3)

I discovered one day that if you divide the chapters of the Bible in half, the chapter in the middle is Psalm 118. Isn't that interesting. I know, it is just a novel thing. I realise the chapters were not in the original writing, so I do not hold this out as theological truth. Just an interesting fact.

There is something else that I thought interesting about that. If you divide the verses in the Bible in half, the verse that comes in the middle occurs in the same psalm, Psalm 118 and it is verse 8. That verse reads

> *it is better to trust in the Lord than to put your confidence in men.*

The Amorite spirit declares that it can depend on anything rather than God. But the Spirit of the Living God says we should depend on nothing outside of the living God and says, let us keep putting our confidence in God. Trust in the Lord rather than in anything or anyone else. The psalmist declares that the right hand of the Lord exalts. The same right hand of the Lord does valiantly. The Lord, who is my strength and my song. The Lord, who is my salvation. The Lord, who watches over me. He is the one who opens to me the gates of righteousness, so I might enter in to His presence. No wonder the psalmist declares,

> *"I will praise You, For you alone are worthy of my praise. This is the Lord's doing. It's marvelous in his eyes. This is the day the Lord is made. I will rejoice and be glad in it" Psalm 118:23-24*

There it is right in the middle of the whole of the Bible the truth which is right in the centre of God's plan and purpose for us; that we might trust in Him rather than anything else. He alone is trustworthy, faithful, true and full of kindness and mercy.

The last thing to say about the Amorite mindset is this. Whenever we start to think that we have achieved something, and arrived at a position of prominence, we should remember that all God is looking for, is a humble and a contrite spirit. Somebody who will bow themselves before Him, knowing they are far from perfect but cast themselves, in their imperfection and sin, upon the goodness, mercy and grace of God.

The world wants to tell us we are special because of who we are. But we are not. We are special because of who God made us to be. The world wants to try and tell us that we need to be famous, to push ourself above everybody else, and become important, to think of ourself as prominent. The living God says, All that we are, that is worthy of note is what He made us. All that we have, that is worthy of note is what He gave us. All that we could ever hope to be, that will count in eternity, is what Jesus alone can do for us and in us.

As for prominence and importance, let us finish by hearing again one of the paradoxes of Jesus the Christ, who in Himself should have been the most prominent, but came as a servant leader, as an example to all His followers to avoid the Amorite spirit. Here He is speaking to His followers

> *And Jesus called them to him and said to them, "You know that those who are considered rulers of the Gentiles lord it over them, and their great ones exercise authority over them. But it shall not be so among you. But whoever would be great among you must be your servant, and whoever would be first among you must be slave of all. For even the Son of Man came not to be served but to serve, and to give his life as a ransom for many."*
> *Mark 10:42-45*

The Amorite spirit is high as a cedar. It is as strong as an oak. But the Lord God will cut the top off and destroy the root, in order to ensure we walk humbly before Him today, and until we come before Him face to face. Until we hear Him say, "Come in. Well done, good and faithful servant." Then even there, we will come in humility and fall on our faces and worship Him for ever.

Jebusites

The names of these giant nations are not just chance names. They are given by the Lord, our God to help us understand the attitudes, the ways of life, and the mindsets, which crop up in our days with the aim of making us lose our focus on God and wander from Him. The enemy desires to keep us away from walking into the promises and favour of the God, who has called us into life and loved us with an everlasting love. The seventh and last of these tribes of giants, is no different in this aim and purpose. This seventh nation Moses and Joshua speak about are the Jebusites.

The Jebusite spirit will not normally be the kind of giant to attack anyone tempted by the Amorite spirit, for where the Amorites mindset seeks to puff us up and bring us to a place where we are looking for fame, prestige, and prominence for ourselves, the Jebusite spirit takes those who are at the opposite end of the confidence scale. It comes to attack those who are struggling to see any value whatsoever in themselves.

It seems that as Joshua sorted this list of giant nations out for us, he set the order very deliberately. He started with the Canaanites, who were the origin of all of the other nations in his list. Then he spoke about irrational terror. After that he took a pair of giant nations which spoke about the problems of either living with over strict limitations and boundaries or with no boundaries, and then the last two nations deal with a similar issue but from the opposite ends of the human psyche. The temptations which face the extrovert and those which the introvert is likely to struggle with. Between the two pairs of giant nations, Joshua drew attention to the nation which seeks to make us live without any thought of God, that nation which encourages us to live as animals, allowing every animalistic instinct to prevail and convince us we are just creatures of time, and not of eternity.

Turning then to this seventh nation, which seems to speak to the issues of the introvert and of a low self esteem, we discover that the first and most obvious meaning of the word Jebusite is 'to bring low', or 'to cast down'.

This nation of giants comes against us in order to bring us to a place where we are left feeling low. You may never have been brought low. You may never have been cast down. You may have just had one of those lives where every day seems to be a great day, and every day seems to be filled with excitement and great thrills. You may be among that group of people who always seem to be uplifted and happy. But most of us live our lives on what appear to be a roller coaster of emotions. Just as we get to the top and think things are sorted out we suddenly find ourselves sinking back down into depths of sorrow and despair. Most of us seem to go up and then sink back down again.

There are thoughts that come into our lives, attitudes that spring up in our lives, which seem determined to try and bring us to a point where we are tempted to just give up. There are some who never seem to be anything but cast down. It is that thought of giving up, and of being cast down which so often is evidence of the Jebusite attack on our minds, whether it comes as a constant condition, or as an occasional thought.

Most of us know days in life when it seems everything is conspiring to make us feel that all we have done was a waste of time. When that happens it can quickly move us to thinking we may as well give up on what we are seeking to do in life. It leads us to think it is time to move on and try something different because everything seems pointless and worthless, achieving nothing. There are even days when we can feel tempted to give up on life itself!

When one of those days comes into our life, we need to see that we are facing a giant we need to slay. We are dealing with a Jebusite giant, who is coming against us to bring us low, to cast us down and if possible to destroy us and even devastate all we have sought to do for God.

As the Jebusite giant comes, he will use phrases like this. "You are no good". "You're a waste of space". "You'll never be any good". "You'll never achieve anything". "You might as well give up now, you will never amount to anything and your life will never count for anything."

Sometimes we find Jebusites coming ostensibly to teach us and help us. They suggest all they are trying to do is spur us into action with their deprecating statements.

There are even times when they come under a religious guise, telling us they are just trying to keep us in a place of humility. All too often their aim is to humiliate us rather than create a true biblical humility within us. There is a world of difference between the two. God will help to keep us humble, but will never humiliate one of His own. The Jebusite really only seeks to humiliate, that he may bring us down, and keep us low, with the aim of destroying our life.

The Jebusite giant not only come to bring us low. One of his other methods is to work on us to create low self esteem, and establish within us a low self image. They will suggest we have little worth, and make us concerned about how others see us. This creation of a low self image is also sometimes achieved through a sense of our physical attributes. It seeks to convince us we are the wrong size, the wrong body shape, the wrong person to meet with others. The aim is always the same, the Jebusite is out to destroy.

When we have a low opinion of ourselves, and struggle with low self esteem, we are unlikely to achieve anything of the purpose and potential that God created for us to know and experience.

This Jebusite spirit is rampant in our day, for these kind of feelings and mindsets are hugely common, especially it seems among younger people. One of the ploys used is to make us think that we are alone with these kinds of feelings and thoughts, and that nobody else will understand. The truth is, when we face a Jebusite spirit, we are facing something common to man across the world and throughout time.

If we were to open a tabloid newspaper or pick up a

woman's magazine, or even a men's magazine, they have numerous letters from people struggling in life, because of a poor self image, and low self esteem. All too often it seems, the writers do not think there is any reason to go on with life. Convinced everything that happens seems to be bad, or everything is hopeless in their life, or that life itself seems a waste of time, and all they have done has come to nothing.

As we read the answers to those letters, it becomes apparent the world has no real answer to the problems expressed. It has no answer, because the world has not diagnosed the real problem. Most of the people who write the letters have been attacked by a Jebusite giant, and have not realized they were meant to slay that giant.

Even if they were to recognise this as the activity of one of the giant nations, many still struggle, for in reality, none of us has any hope against this giant if we are standing and fighting in our own strength. The giant is bigger, mightier, stronger, greater, and more powerful than we are. They will bring us low, they will cast us down they will increase the loss of self worth until they win! But in the strength of the living God, every giant that comes against us, can fall, they can be destroyed, and we can discover that the bigger they are the harder they will fall.

The name Jebusite starts with this idea of 'casting down', 'bringing low'. Yet there is far more than that included in the meaning of this word. If you study out the name Jebusite it has two distinct branches of meaning in the root of the name. Both of them have this aim and purpose of casting down and bringing low.

The first one has within it the idea of threshing. If you've ever watched a threshing machine at work, they work to beat the harvested item. It used to be done by hand, but the idea is the same whether by hand or machine, threshing has to do with beating. When the cut plant is beaten down, two elements are left. First there is the grain, which is valuable, that part of the plant which was the reason for the threshing. Then there is the waste product, the chaff. When the grain is separated from the chaff it would be ground down under a heavy weighted stone.

This word Jebusite has both these idea of first threshing and then grinding. There are some things that come into our experience that just bring us low. There are other things that come into life which make us feel as though we have been beaten to a pulp. Then there are some things in life which after making us feel beaten down, takes any tiny part which seems to have been left unscathed and places it under a weight grinding it to dust. Like a millstone that grinds long and grinds slow, grinding until there is nothing left.

To be crushed under pressure, crushed to a place where there appears to be no way out leaves us in a situation where we can get so low, that we actually see no way out, and whichever way we look, it seems as though we are between a rock and a hard place. Under pressure, being brought low, and crushed.

That is the first branch of meaning which is in the root of this word Jebusite. To be bought to a place where we think we have nothing, and can achieve nothing. It speaks of those situations in life that come to brings us down, and achieves that purpose through a kind of crushing weight laid upon us until we feel there is no hope and no escape.

Then secondly within the name Jebusite is the idea of something polluted. I always wonder how much of anything has to be added to something else before it has polluted it.

I remember going one day to a place where there was a spring of water, and next to the spring there was a plaque erected which said that the water out of the spring was completely pure. The people who lived there used to take that water and do their washing in it. They used to let the water come out of the spring run a little into the stream and then wash in the water. It was possible to stand and look into the water and see every stone on the bottom of the stream. I was told the people in the village used the water to do their washing in. The water was so pure, that river eels and a number of other animals lived in it. Then a little further down the stream there was a notice to say you could draw the water and it was pure enough to drink and cook with.

I was not sure just how clean the water was. I did not know how pure the water really was, but I did know that even if it was clean enough and pure enough to drink as it came out of the spring, I would not want to drink it after it had passed the place where people washed in it, where animals lived in it, and where the washing had been done. But I was told that as the water passes along the stones it makes it clean. Maybe it does, but there seemed too much opportunity for pollution to encourage me to try drinking from that place. How much of anything does it take to pollute and ruin something until it is becomes no longer safe, or useable?

I wonder whether you have ever gone into a petrol station and been preoccupied, in some way and finished up putting the wrong kind of fuel into your car. I confess I have done it. My mind has been elsewhere and without thinking I have added petrol to a diesel car. I stopped very quickly, but not before I had added a few litres of the wrong fuel. I went and asked the garage what could be done, only to be told there was no option but to call someone to drain the tank completely. Without doing this the small amount of petrol, would so pollute the diesel that the car would not run and the engine would be ruined beyond repair. I made the call and waited for the specialist to arrive to drain the fuel tank.

Once the tank had been emptied the specialist added some diesel and then emptied the tank again, then they put some diesel in, and emptied it a third time, then they put some diesel in, tested the engine and told me they thought the car should now be safe to drive.

I asked how much of the petrol would it take to pollute the diesel. They told me it only takes about a teaspoonful in 60 litres of diesel to pollute the diesel to the stage where it becomes likely to damage the engine. Now that is a little tiny pollution, but even that small pollution can destroy everything.

This word Jebusite has this idea of pollution within the root of the name. This giant will beat us down, put us into a situation where life seems of little worth, bring us to a place of low self esteem where we think we are worthless, and incapable of anything worthwhile. He will seek to crush us under the weight of circumstances, under the problems of our days. Then, when we are low, and not thinking straight about ourself or our life, he will seek to pollute our very heart and mind with something. Only the slightest little pollution.

Once that pollution has an entry, this Jebusite giant will keep reminding us of the pollution. He will suggest that even if we think it is a very little, tiny pollution, it is still enough to destroy us. He will try to convince us that God will give up on us and never own us again. It is that thought of God giving up on us, which should convince us all this is coming from an enemy and not from the convicting work of God the Holy Spirit.

Always understand, the Jebusite, in common with all these other giant nations, has our destruction in mind. They want to turn us off from God. They want to keep us from the promises that God has put into our life and into His word. So the Jebusite will try to get us to allow just a little pollution into our life, with the aim that at every moment of the day, he can come and remind us of the pollution that he might destroy us, that he might crush us and that he might thresh and grind us to dust.

The Jebusite giants come to tell us we are worth nothing. They will use the falls and failings in our life to help to enforce the message that we are worthless. These enemies will tell us, we have messed up, ruined everything, and that things are so bad there is no way for us to ever come back to God. They want to remove all hope and leave us in absolute despair.

The truth is that every one of the giant enemies are liars, like their father, the enemy of souls, who himself has been a liar from the very beginning. However low we feel, whatever we have done that we think has polluted our being, how ever small our self esteem is, there is a way into God's presence and there is a way to overcome every enemy of our souls.

It starts like this. The Jebusite will tell us, we are worth nothing. That is his first lie. To realise just what we are truly worth to God, we only have to turn our eyes towards the cross of Calvary, to the place where Jesus bled and died for us. Look and consider for a moment, the wounds he bore, gaze on His hands, His feet, and see the Saviour hanging there for you and for me. He paid the price for our sin. The debt we owed to God, that we might know the favour and blessing of the living God.

Understand, remember, never forget, never doubt for a single second, that is how valuable God thinks we are, that is how precious God believes us to be. Any thought of low self esteem, is a denial of the value that God put upon us. Any thought that we cannot do anything worthwhile is a denial of the God who prepared, beforehand, good works for us to do.

The first thing to do, when we hear the Jebusite coming to whisper we are nothing and we will never achieve anything, is to run back to the cross and see the perfect Son of the Father, removing our pollution and dying in our place, because of the worth He placed upon our lives.

Then, whenever the Jebusite comes to remind us that we are polluted, that we really messed up, that we are so bad God can never use us, we must remind ourselves that whether we are faithful or not, God is faithful, He will never go back on His word, or His promise, and His word declares that if we come to Him and confess our pollution, if we tell Him we have sinned, we have really messed up, He, that glorious, holy, perfect, never changing God, is faithful to do all that He has said. When we come like that, not only is He faithful but He is just, and that faithfulness and that justice is demonstrated in Him forgiving us.

That is wonderful all by itself, but God's faithfulness and justice does not stop there. He goes on to declare He will also cleanse us from all unrighteousness.

> *If we confess our sins, he is faithful and just to forgive us our sins and to cleanse us from all unrighteousness. 1 John 1:9*

Every time I read that promise to cleanse from all unrighteousness, I am reminded of the specialist draining the tank, putting some clean, correct fuel in, draining again, adding some more correct clean fuel, draining again until the pollution was completely erased and no evidence is left that any pollution had ever taken place. The removal of the pollution took time, but in the end it was complete.

The third thing we must remember is that this God not only counted us so valuable that He sent His son to redeem us, not only is He determined to remove every stain of pollution and sin, this God declares one day He will take us as His children and set us as one of His jewels.

If you ever talk to a real jeweller, and ask to see some gem stones, they will get out a black cloth and place their gem stone in the centre of the blackness. They do it to show off the way the light catches the facets in the stone. God says when He has finished the work on cleaning us up completely, He will set each of us as His jewels in a way that reflects the light of His glory, the light of His beauty in all that He has made us to be.

It will not be a black background God uses to show off His work within us, when it is finally complete. The prophet Malachi says that God carries us and keeps us and will place us as jewels in His hand. Finally there the full effect of the reflection of His beauty within us will be seen. When Malachi tells us we are to be like a jewel in the hand of God, remember, those are the hands that put the stars in place. God says He holds us in the palm of His hand as jewels, we are not of little worth. Begone unbelief, agree with God. We are of infinite worth. It is why He purchased us. Purchased not with silver or gold but with the precious blood of His son.

> *"They shall be mine, says the LORD of hosts, in the day when I make up my treasured possession, and I will spare them as a man spares his son who serves him. Malachi 3:17*

Then finally understand that when the Jebusite comes and tells us that we are nothing, that we can do nothing, that we will always be a failure, and that our life will always be a mess, it is not a time to argue with him, it is a time to run to God. We must agree with the God who declares that far from being unable to do anything we can do all things with Him and through Christ who is our strength. When the Jebusite tells us, we are not achieving anything, not doing anything worthwhile, we remind ourselves that God has declared that we can do whatever He has asked of us. There is nothing God requires which we cannot do with His help. Our sins are washed away, we are a jewel in God's sight. He counts us as truly precious, and by the indwelling of His spirit and the strength of the risen Christ within us, we are able to fulfil all God has purposed for each one of us.

> *I can do all things through him who strengthens me. Philippians 4:13.*

God declares, He has not only made us His jewels, but He opens all of His treasure to us so that whatever He asks us to do, when we put our hand to accomplish His bidding, He will bless that endeavour. That is a promise from the God who always keeps His word.

> *The LORD will open to you his good treasury, the heavens, to give the rain to your land in its season and to bless all the work of your hands. Deuteronomy 28:12.*

That same God is also able to prosper, to favour and to establish the work of our hands and put His beauty, His splendor, His delight, His value and His grace upon us.

> *Let the favor of the Lord our God be upon us, and establish the work of our hands upon us; yes, establish the work of our hands! Psalm 90:17*

This living God did not just watch us come into the world by chance and then wonder what to do with us. Even before we were in the womb, He knew us. Actually before the world was even created He had set His heart upon us and put a plan in place to bring us to a purpose and to a destiny. We are not just walking through these days with nothing doing for us. We are not a waste of space, we are not a mistake. We are in his hand. He has a purpose and a destiny, and His thoughts are aimed at bringing that purpose to pass. Jeremiah 29:11.

> *For I know the plans I have for you, declares the Lord, plans for welfare and not for evil, to give you a future and a hope. Jeremiah 29:11.*

Since God counts us as valuable and precious, since He sent His Son into the world in order to wash away our sin and make us His jewels, since He has promised to set His hand upon whatever He asks of us which we then set out to do for Him, let us agree with God's estimation and set our hands to work for Him. What we seek to do, let us do with all our might, and do it in the strength and power of the risen Saviour and know we can achieve all that He purposed for us to do if we will only walk in His ways.

Summing up giants

The contention that has birthed this whole book is a simple one. It is based upon an understanding of the Bible which claims that all these things are written for a purpose. The Apostle Paul sets out the purpose of the Old Testament very clearly for us.

> *For whatever was written in former days was written for our instruction, that through endurance and through the encouragement of the Scriptures we might have hope.* Romans 15:4

That understanding has undergirded the whole of my life and ministry. It means that whenever I turn to what is written in the Scripture, especially when it comes to the Old Testament, I come with a presupposition that nothing is there by chance, or by mistake. More than that, I am convinced it is written for the instruction of God's people. I hold that to be the case, even when I read those portions, which at first sight appear to have little relevance to the days we live in. When I read sections like that, I believe it is the limit of our understanding causing us to fail to see meaning and value within them.

With that contention, I set out to discover why these nations of giants were not only listed twice, but many of them are mentioned even more frequently throughout the whole of the Scripture, as the people of God struggled to come to terms with what it meant to walk in the promises of God and fulfil the destiny that God had purposed for them. Time and again, God's people were overcome by their enemies, as they took their eyes away from Him.

Equally, every time they turned their attention back and focussed on living for God and seeking His face and favour, the enemies were defeated. That held true even where the odds against them seemed impossible to overcome. All of that caused me to look specifically at these seven nations of giants, and as I looked into the background of their names, I became amazed that so often those names seemed to speak to exactly the same issues and mindsets people struggle with in the 21st century.

They concerned mindsets that bring people to doubt God, to question God, to turn from God, to walk away from seeking God to fulfil His word and promise in their lives. They spoke to issues that make us settle for less than God's best. I found the nations listed by Moses and Joshua spoke to the problems which are still out there in the world, bringing doubt, fear, destruction, temptation and despair to many people, even the people of God, who ought to know better.

We believe that Jesus the Christ did not just come into the world to save us from our sins, thank God for that incredible and wonderful truth. If all that Jesus ever came to do, was wash our sins away in His own precious blood, that is an amazing thing. But He came to accomplish far more than that. He also came to give us an abundant life, so that we might enjoy life here on the earth, in the way God intended us to enjoy it. He came to ensure that we could live with the indwelling presence of His Spirit, and He came to make it possible for us to enjoy life in the way God will allow us to experience it in the fullness of His presence for eternity.

But there is an enemy who is out to steal, to kill and to destroy. He is the enemy of souls. He comes with many names, and he comes in a variety of guises and with a host of his fallen cohorts. These seven nations each come and represent a different ploy, a change of tactic which Satan will use in his warfare against us.

These seven nations speak of the seduction of stuff, materialism, the onset of phobias, fear and terror. They speak of the danger of living without vision, and of living without the restraints and the restrictions set by God. They speak of the danger of pride, desiring recognition and fame for yourself, and also of the tragedy of living with low self esteem. They speak of the absurdity of thinking we are just another species of animal and the folly of living in a purely carnal fashion, and of the dangers of humanism that flow from that, living with no thought of eternity.

One or more of these nations of giants will dog your feet. As you read the book, you will have recognized his steps, and recalled his whisper in your ears. You may even have recollected the time you heard him shout into your life that anything was better than trying to live for God. All they ever say is a lie.

As we come towards a close there are three things that we do well to set in place in our hearts and minds as we seek to do battle with the enemy and these giant nations.

The first thing is a conviction we all need to know something about the enemies devices, about the kind of schemes he will use, about the plans he is seeking to bring to pass, and above all what Satan is thinking as he comes to attack you and attempt to take you away from God.

A day will come when we will no longer be troubled by any giants who dog our footsteps, but in this life, each of us tends to find ourselves susceptible to one or another of these giants. More than that, by our own selves we give away to the enemy where our particular weakness lies.

The Apostle Paul wrote to the church in Corinth and said he wanted them all to know, to be aware of, to not be ignorant of, the devices and schemes of the enemy, to be cognisant of the way he thinks, of the kind of plans he makes, and of the manner of traps he will lay in order to try to bring them down. Writing in 2 Corinthians 2:11 he explained that the enemy is trying to outwit even him. We are in a fight.

Writing to the Ephesian church, that same Apostle said:

> *we do not wrestle against flesh and blood, but against the rulers, against the authorities, against the cosmic powers over this present darkness, against the spiritual forces of evil in the heavenly places. Ephesians 6:12*

Too many want to put the full stop and finish the sentence earlier than the Apostle. All too often we tend to wish it just said, "we do not wrestle" and stopped there. But we are in a fight. If we fail to realise that, or we ignore the ploys of the enemy, we will find ourselves attacked by one of these nations and wonder whatever has happened. Some of us even think at that moment, that we never signed up to be in a fight. But from Genesis through to

Revelation, God explains we are in a battle and that we need to have some understanding of the method and motive of the enemy.

We should also remember from that text in Ephesians that it is not human individuals we are fighting. These nations were certainly nations of humans, but they are not recorded for us to lead us to fight people. The real forces who are coming against us, as God's people are spiritual giants, even if they use individuals to seek to fulfil their purposes. Do not be misled into fighting the wrong foe. Understand also these spiritual forces come against us, not just to destroy us, but through their strategy against us, to oppose God Himself. It is God they stand against.

Within the scripture God has given us the tools we need to slay those giants, with His help and strength. We are made to be overcomers, more than conquerors, victorious in the fight. Over the chapters of this book we have looked at some of the tools given to us to fight whenever the giants comes toward us. All too often we would rather run from the fight than stand in the strength of God. We must learn to stand and having done all to still stand.

I wonder if you have ever noticed this story:

> *And Benaiah the son of Jehoiada was a valiant man of Kabzeel, a doer of great deeds. He struck down two champions of Moab. He also went down and struck down a lion in a pit on a day when snow had fallen. 2 Samuel 23:20*

The same story, probably unknown to many, is also recorded in 1 Chronicles 11. This man, Benaiah, whose name means "built up by Jehovah" was the son of Jehoida. His fathers name means "God knows where you're at." What an incredible heritage to have and what an amazing name to be given. To come from the one of whom it can be said, God knows where you are at, and then you are given a name as a reminder that you are built up by Jehovah God.

This man was one of David's valiant men. We are told that he struck down a lion, he slew a lion. That is quite a feat of strength and valour all on it's own. Then we are told how he did that. He chased a lion and when the lion fell into the pit, he chased down after the lion into the pit. Finally we are given the weather conditions as we are told this happened in the snow.

When we begin to look at that verse we might be tempted to think it a strange thing to do. When we see a lion, we do not think about the lion in the same way as the lion may think about us. The lion may well look at us and think we are his lunch. Understand lions can run at about 30-35 miles an hour. So when we see a lion we may be tempted to run and try to hide. After all, it is unlikely we could manage to out run the lion. We might be tempted to think our only hope to run would come if we happen to be with another person who is unable to run as fast as we can.

What we are told here is that this man, Beniah, whose life had been built up by God, saw a lion, and rather than run, he chased towards it. So here is the picture. There is a lion running down the road and this man is running down behind it with his weapon in his hand. We are not told whether he had a sword, or a club or just his bare hands. We are just told he is running, and the snow has fallen.

In the snow the lion slipped and fell in a pit. Now when the lion has fallen into a pit and it is there in the snow, what would we be inclined to do? What the scripture says is, straight after the lion's paw prints went into the pit, a set of human foot prints followed in the snow. Before too long, there is just one set of footprints coming out of the pit. That single set of prints coming back out, do not belong to the lion but to this man whose name and testimony was "God built me up".

Read the story as it appears there in 2 Samuel, and understand the context of the story. David is choosing his mighty men of valor. This is King David. He is the man who as a youth came and saw a giant called Goliath standing in the bottom of the valley, shouting at the people of God and saying, "I don't believe in your God, your God can't do anything. I'll tell you what, you are finished people. You are destroyed. People you're on your own." Then remember that, faced with the giant Goliath, David said "let me take him out". He took one look at the giant, and while everyone else was wanting to run the other way, David ran down the hill, with the name, the power, and the strength of the living God. He also carried a sling, and five stones. With all that, David slew Goliath. That David looked at Benaiah and said, this is the kind of man I can have on my side.

But I want you to know why the story is there. Why the only thing we know about this man are the two short references. Beniah's name is mentioned again, but every other time it is just his name that is included.

He went out and killed a lion, in the snow. In other words, when everything seemed to be set against him, when all the odds weighed heavily against him, he went out and killed what came to destroy him.

The God who ensured that story would form a few verses in the Old Testament is the same God who inspired the Apostle Peter to write his letter to the scattered believers. In that letter he wrote about their need to know the adversary and recognise the way he is and one of the ways he comes against us. He writes, the devil is prowling around looking for you. He wants to take you away from God. He wants to destroy the faith you have. He wants to chew you up and spit you out and leave you ruined.

> *Be sober-minded; be watchful. Your adversary the devil prowls around like a roaring lion, seeking someone to devour. Resist him, firm in your faith, knowing that the same kinds of suffering are being experienced by your brotherhood throughout the world. 1 Peter5:8-9*

Normally our reaction on seeing a lion coming to attack, would be to run away, and certainly there are times when a good run, is better than a bad stand. The Apostle Peter, however, looking at the lion coming says we should not run but resist, standing firm in our faith. When these giants come, it is not the time to run in flight. It is a time to stand and fight.

We may be tempted to think it is in our nature to run and be afraid. Fear, we may think, is natural. We are scared of so many things. We excuse ourselves and say, it is just human to be afraid, but the truth is, we were never made to be afraid.

Medical science tells us that when a baby is born it is scared of only two things. They are scared of great noise, and they are scared of falling. The world specialists who study such things believe that from the time we are born to the time we die, we have the chance of getting anything up to 2000 other fears in our lives. Without wishing to belittle anyone, or make light of those fears, the scientists tell us those 2000 fears have been categorised. There is even a very real fear some have of peanut butter sticking on the roof of their mouth. There are some who go through life scared to love. Some who are terrified their life will end, so terrified they cannot enjoy the days they have. We noticed much of this as we thought about the Hittites giants.

Out of those 2000 phobias, only those two things frightened us when we were born. Every other fear is a fear we have learned. God never put those learned fears within us. They all came from somewhere else. God never gave us a spirit of fear. If we learned those other fears, we must be able to learn how to live unafraid. It is why the Scriptures have so many references that say "fear not".

One man could stand against a lion, and in the strength of the living God, he managed to slay that lion. David discovered, when he ran down into the valley, with his five small stones and his one sling, that in the strength of God, he was able to hit a giant, and then cut the head off that giant. Understand you and I can also discover that the God we worship is the God who also said, I will drive those giants out before you, and deliver them into your hand. It is time to take a stand and slay the giant that is coming to attack you.

When the Apostle Peter uses the word "resist" it is the word which means 'to stand and fight'. When he uses the word 'steadfast' he uses a word which means 'do not move your ground.' When he says 'in our faith' he is reminding us we cannot do any of this in our own strength, but we can do it, in the strength of the living God. When we stand our ground against the giant coming against us, God will drive him before us, we can run after him in the strength of that living God, and destroy the giant. It takes faith, and it takes courage. General George Patton was asked what courage was and he said "Courage is this, coping with your fear for one minute more. Going on for one more minute."

But when we go to war against the giant, remember it is the giant we need to slay. Be careful not to kill the wrong thing. It is the thought pattern, the attitude, the way of thinking, the paradigm that governs your life, which we are to destroy. Kill the wrong thought processes, correct the false mindsets, change the paradigm to a godly one.

To enable us to kill those wrong thought patterns, those dangerous attitudes, the false paradigms that try to invade our thinking, God has given us weapons. They are not carnal weapons.

> *For though we walk in the flesh, we are not waging war according to the flesh. For the weapons of our warfare are not of the flesh but have divine power*

> *to destroy strongholds. We destroy arguments and every lofty opinion raised against the knowledge of God, and take every thought captive to obey Christ, being ready to punish every disobedience, when your obedience is complete.*
>
> 2 Corinthians 10:3-6

The Apostle Paul comes to the church in Corinth and tells them that the weapons God has put into our hands are powerful, they are strong, they are mighty. Then he speaks about the ability of these weapons 'to destroy', to pull down and to demolish. Then he says they destroy 'arguments and every lofty opinion', the words he uses refer to thought processes and patterns. So that what Paul writes is something like this. "There are things that can take hold of your mind. They want to mould your mind and make it think in a certain way and in a certain direction. But we have weapons that are spiritual weapons, which we can use to enable us to demolish every stronghold and argument that comes against our mind, and to bring down the thought pattern that has been set against us."

These giants are attitudes, they are ways of thinking, they are thought processes, they are world views. They are not people. These giants come and drip things into our brain to try and make us think in ways that will move us from God. Paul says we have spiritual weapons to cast down and destroy those thought patterns. Paul says that when the giant comes, God has given us all we need to change our way of thinking into the way God wants us to think. We can overcome the thought patterns that the giant brings and wants us to think. Both God and the giants are aware 'that as a man thinks in his heart, so is he.'

Paul says we need to bring every thought captive to obey Christ. How many thoughts do we have in a day. The weapon we have, is the weapon of taking every one of those thoughts captive to obey Christ. Consciously then, as thoughts come, as attitudes come, as ways of thinking occur to us, we need to take each thought to Jesus.

If that means nothing else, it has to mean that every minute, I am to be found running and speaking to the living God and remembering the wonder of who Jesus is and the glory and miracle of all that He did for me. It must intend we should spend our moments day by day with Jesus in the forefront of our lifes. All that will require us to learn to think differently.

Transformed thinking

To close this whole book, we could have thought about a number of different aspects of spiritual warfare, but my main emphasis has been on the attack that the giants bring to our minds and our way of thinking. The Apostle Paul was conscious in each of his letters that the attack from the enemy is against the mind. The Apostle Peter also drew attention to the need to be sober minded; to think aright in 1 Peter 5:8. They both saw the battle as a fight which the enemy seeks to bring to our minds. So in closing these chapters I want to think about words of the Apostle Paul at the start of Romans 12 where he speaks of the way our minds need to be changed.

Paul has written to the christians in Rome, and by chapter twelve he has completed the portion of his letter which covers christian doctrine, theological teaching, the truths of the gospel. He has dealt with those things in the first eleven chapters. He unpacked those gospel truths with two turning points, one at the start of chapter 5 where he writes 'Therefore, we have peace with God.' The second is at the start of chapter 8 where he writes 'Therefore, there is no condemnation.' He finished that doctrinal section of the letter in the way he often did, with a doxology, a prayer. In Romans that comes at the close of chapter 11 with a prayer about the wonder, the majesty, the glory, the wisdom, the boundless goodness of God.

Then he turns to talk about practical issues, practical considerations which flow from the gospel truths he has elaborated on and that he trusts have been understood by his readers. This is what he then writes:

> *I appeal to you therefore, brothers, by the mercies of God, to present your bodies as a living sacrifice, holy and acceptable to God, which is your spiritual worship. Do not be conformed to this world, but be transformed by the renewal of your mind, that by testing you may discern what is the will of God, what is good and acceptable and perfect.*
> *Romans 12:1-2*

I remember, even now, the first time these two verses began to really impact my heart and mind. I was sitting in a seminar at St Anne's College, in Oxford. The sessions were being run under the auspices of the King's University in America, and the seminar was being led by Bishop Ulmer. We took three days to look through these two verses, and I began not only to be impacted by Paul's teaching, but also by the truth that every word was here for a reason. Every day I left and spent the journey home in tears longing to know; not just what the words meant but what the experience Paul was asking us to seek, would look like in my life.

I ask you now to look with me at the words Paul uses in these two verses, and allow them to impact your mind and thinking, as I share some of the lessons I learned in those seminars, about the meaning of each word.

Paul sets out a foundation for the way the gospel should affect us if we belong to Jesus the Christ. He says it is all down to the mind. He is going to go on to deal with all sorts of differing issues and problems but he sets this foundation statement, that if the mind is right, everything else will follow. The way we think, will always affects the way we act.

When we are talking about the mind, understand, we are not just talking about an intellectual thought process. We are thinking about everything we think, feel and do, since all of that starts with the brain, and the way our brains are trained and process everything in life.

Whenever you see the word 'therefore' always remember it is 'there for' a reason. The apostle is asking us to think about what has gone before. He is asking us to look back and think about what has been said so far. He is about to set out the reasons why we should allow the way we think, and therefore act, to be adjusted. He says we should think about the mercies of God, of all that Jesus the Christ has done for us, all that He gave for us, all He endured for us, all He won for us. How He left the realms of glory, walked in purity and perfection on the face of this earth was mocked, scorned, scourged, beaten, crucified, dead, taken down, put in a tomb, and rose again and all for us. Because as we allow ourselves to spend time thinking of all that, it will make us comprehend the plea he is about to make.

Paul makes a plea, it is a plea, an appeal, an entreaty, not a command. Paul never says we must do this. There may be some who wish to make this a command. Some may even think the apostle meant to write this as a direct instruction. But Paul does not say, "if you don't do this, you're out the door." Instead he appeals, he beseeches, he asks and invites us to think about all that Jesus has done and then think about his next request.

This word translated 'appeal' is a word which means he is telling his readers he is coming alongside them and asking them to do what he asks so that they all might be standing together with him.

The word comes from the verb 'parakaleo'. The noun form of that word is the greek word 'paraclete'. Every one of his original readers would have known he was using a word that would create a connection in their minds to the person of the Holy Spirit. He does this in order to remind them that what he is about to ask, they will never be able to do alone, they would only be able to do this with the aid of one standing alongside them, the paraclete. They would need God the Holy Spirit to help them in this.

So you could say Paul wrote something that he intended to be read like this: 'I am appealing to you, and remember the Holy Spirit is there within you, if you are saved. He is there dwelling in the midst of your being, and He is there help you do this, He is there to come alongside and lead you. I want to remind you, you need the promised help of the Holy Spirit to do what I am asking you to do. That promised help will come alongside, He will also make this same plea and will guide you into the right way so we stand together.'

Paul's plea is that his readers should think of all that God has done in mercy and on their behalf, and then, in the light of all this, present their bodies to God. He asks them to do something with the body they live in, which includes their mind and their will. He asks them to present all that to God.

We tend to read this word 'present' as though it is merely asking us to bring and show, or maybe bring and give to God. But when we read it like that, we completely miss the meaning and the intention of the apostle.

The greek word Paul uses is a very specific verb, used in a very specific tense. The tense Paul uses is the aorist tense. The aorist is used of an action done once, and only once, because when it is done once it cannot be done again. We need to understand first that Paul is asking us to do something, which once done, we will never need do again. It will be settled and finished once and for all.

Then the verb translated by this word 'present' is a word which was a uniquely technical term used in the temples. It is a term his readers in Rome would have understood from their temple worship. They would have understood it in that way whether they were jew or gentile, since both groups knew what was done as in their temples where the worship involved presenting something.

Our problem is when we read it we do not have that background of sacrificial worship in temples, and so we fail to fully comprehend the extent and power of what the apostle is suggesting. We live in a different world.

The word is a technical term referring to what happened when you bought an item with the aim of offering it to your god, whoever that god was. The term refers to the act of coming and bringing your sacrificial item. The offerer would make his way towards the temple with their offering but as yet they had not presented their gift. They would walk into the temple with their gift, but they still had not presented it. They would bring their offering to the priest, still it had not been presented. They may even have helped to lay their offering on the altar, but still their offering had not been presented.

The word 'present' refers to the time when the offering had been brought to the temple, laid on the altar, given over to the control of the priest. Only when the hands of the offerer were removed from their offering and they had neither access or control over the gift, then and only then had their gift been truly presented.

Paul is asking us to do that with our life. To take our lives, body, mind, and will, and place it in the hands of the living God, commit it to the Holy Spirit who dwells within, and relinquish any rights of control or rule over any of it.

Paul is wanting us to come and realise we have had enough of trying to do things our way. We relinquish all control and governance over our beings. We take our hands off the choices, the desires, the plans and the control of our days, and we begin to live by the leading and lordship of God the Holy Spirit. We do that once, never again to seize control and usurp the throne of our lives from Him whose we are, and who purchased us at such great cost to Himself.

All to Jesus I surrender,
All to Him I freely give;
I will ever love and trust Him,
In His presence daily live.

All to Jesus I surrender,
Humbly at His feet I bow,
Worldly pleasures all forsaken;
Take me, Jesus, take me now.

All to Jesus I surrender, make me,
Saviour, wholly Thine;
Let me feel Thy Holy Spirit,
Truly know that Thou art mine.

All to Jesus I surrender,
Lord, I give myself to Thee;
Fill me with Thy love and power,
Let Thy blessing fall on me.
Judson W. Van De Venter

Paul appeals for us to think of what Jesus did for us and then to bring all we are and all we have, and hand complete control of it all to God,. Then he adds that we are to do this by way of a living sacrifice.

Normally, when you presented your gift to your god in the temple, your sacrifice was put to death. Paul asks us instead to put our life, body, mind, will, indeed our everything into the hands of God, for him to do with us, as he chooses, recognising that we no longer have control over the choices of what to do with our body, mind, will, our flesh, understanding as we relinquished control, God would never kill us, but chooses to bless us and use us for His own purposes and glory.

Paul's aim is that all of us should live our lives under the lordship of God, and that living in this way our lives might be lived in such a way as to reflect the glory, wonder and majesty of the God who saved us and whose purpose is to make us holy. God's aim, when we give Him our all is to make us a reflection of what He is like. That we might walk in holiness, purity and completeness, lacking nothing. It is with this in mind that Paul adds the statement that doing this is 'holy and acceptable unto God'.

Now the word 'holy' is a word which speaks of being set apart. Being set apart includes two things. We are set apart from something and we are also set apart to something. We are set apart from that which we used to do, from what used to be the old manner and style of life we lived under the control of the world's mindset. Those old habits have to disappear, those old ways have to vanish from our life. We are released from these as we release control over ourselves, and hand that control to God. We are released from our old ways.

At the same time we are set apart to something. We are set apart to God, that God might have the control over all that we are, all that we do, all that we say, and all that we think.

Paul says, living like that is not only pleasing to God it is the only acceptable worship and reasonable service we can ever offer to God.

The word translated as 'reasonable', in some versions is translated 'spiritual', but the best translation of the word Paul uses is found in the english term 'logical'.

Giving total control of our life to God, as a response to all that Jesus has done for us, is the only logical thing to do. Jesus held nothing back. Giving our all to God is the only logical response we can make. Holding nothing back. Jesus saved us from the life we once had, which was a life, set on a path to death and destruction. The only logical response is to come to Him, thank Him and bring everything we are and all that we have and place it all in the hands of God, to do with as He pleases. This is not only logical, it is the only logical worship and service we can bring in response to God's mercy and grace.

The question occurs 'how can we give it all to God? What does that look like? How is that achieved?' I struggled with those questions for months. Yet in the second verse Paul tells us how all this can be accomplished.

He tells us not to be conformed, but instead to be transformed, in the way we think. He want us to understand that living the Christian life in the kingdom is significantly an intellectual exercise. It is not mainly about our feelings, or our emotions, though these will be affected, this christian life is all about our thinking. We have to allow God to change the way we think.

The world is trying to make us conform. It is trying to mould us, to shape us, constantly seeking to bring us into the world system, the mindset of worldly ways, the paradigms of the giants. The power of the evil one is constantly seeking to adjust our thinking so that it is in line with the mood and method of the world he controls. He is trying to let the world systems influence our mind and as a result to govern our actions. He brings this influence by what we listen to, by what we look at, and by what we give our attention to.

One of the ways the evil one will popularise sin, is to make it appear less serious, to allow us to laugh at it. We may even find sin works it's way, and is represented as quite normal in story lines in the media. Slowly what once was considered to be unthinkable becomes not just acceptable but common.

Invariably, we think, in the way we have been taught to think. We think, and our minds our trained to think, by what we spend time and give attention to. From the youngest age we go into the school system. From that early stage the attack on the mind begins to mould the way we think. It continues right the way through college or university. When our youngsters go to university, they need to make sure they have Jesus before they get there, because they surely will not normally find Him there.

The world system is trying to configure the way we think and destroy any effort to think spiritually. Paul says we need to ensure we do not let the world shape our way of thinking. Rather than allowing the world to mould our thinking, we need to be transformed, in our thinking.

The word Paul uses which is translated by this word 'transformed' is a word which has come straight from the greek into common english language. It is the word 'metamorphosis."

Metamorphosis is what happens when a caterpillar goes to sleep in the winter. It goes to bed as a caterpillar. It emerges the next spring as a butterfly. Somewhere in the intervening months it metamorphosed.

The verb Paul uses is grammatically passive. It is a word which speaks of something done to you. It is a word that speaks of the work of God, the Holy Spirit, coming into the heart and into the mind to change the way we think. He can do that, only when we have given over control and management of all our moments to Him.

Now, if we are metamorphosed and the word is passive, we may wonder whether we are engaged in doing anything, or whether once we hand over control to God we need do nothing more at all.

That kind of letting go and letting God with no part for us to engage in would be to misunderstand this picture and would be quite wrong. We need to be active and engaged, not in the metamorphosis but in the next verb which he uses, the 'renewing' of our minds.

He says, as the Holy Spirit works within us, we start to think the things of God, we start to think the words of God. That determination to think the words and ways which God puts before our minds and in our lives is involved in this renewing of our minds. It is to make our minds think new things. But It is 'renewed', because when God made man, He gave him the ability to think the thoughts of God. That ability was lost when Adam fell, but it is made new again and restored when a life is handed over to God. This renewing of our thinking is our part in the process.

As we think about God, and as we bring into play, what God has done for us, and think about how we can reflect what God has done for us, in the way we live, God the Holy Spirit will take that metamorphosed thinking He has put into our minds and begin to make us a holy people, set apart from what we used to be, set apart holy and wholly to God. It will change our opinions and our choices. Then instead of making our opinions and choices based on what the world says, we begin to allow our opinions, our choices and our whole way of thinking to be based solely on what God says.

We take the thinking of God, we take the heart of God, and we start to allow God to help us apply that into all the different situations and circumstances we face. We stop being moulded by the giants that come against us. We get back to the Word of God and start to think differently. We begin to realize our minds need to discern the will of God. We allow our cognitive ability to make choices based on the truth of God, on what God says. We concentrate and comprehend the things of the Spirit and the things of eternity. We can only do this as saved people, christian people, for in our relationship with God we have been given the mind of Christ.

Our goal is not to fit Jesus into our lives. He does not want space in our life. He wants all of our life. He never comes to fit in, He only ever comes to take over. It is not that we should fit the ways of God into our life. We are instead intended to order our life around the relationship we have with God, to order our lives, not with Jesus as a useful addition, but as the total reason for anything and everything in life.

Uncommitted lives, were never God's intention. His intention, when He gave His Son for us was that He might be the center of all that we are, of all that we think and of all that we do.

God will have all of our heart, all of our mind, all of our soul, all of our life.

> *"What is religion but seeking God, inquiring after him, applying to him upon all occasions? We make nothing of our religion, if we do not make heart-work of it; God will have all the heart, or none. Our devotedness to God our Saviour, should be avowed and shown in the most solemn and public manner." Matthew Henry writing on the story of Asa in 2 Chronicles 15.*

When that becomes true for us, our minds will begin to be transformed, and our ability to renew our thinking will increase. We will begin to be changed. In renewing the way we think we will begin to see victories and conquests of issues thoughts and habits we thought would never be able to change and one by one the giants will fall.

My prayer in writing this book is just this. That reader and writer alike will all come to the place where God is our all in all.